ENDORSEMENTS

Kim Marxhausen's book is a gift to all caregivers trying to navigate through a difficult season of life. The book is organized by topics that focus on issues of emotional health. Some chapters are specific for those caring for a loved one with memory challenges, and others are for caregiving in general. Each section ends with discussion questions, a reflection on God's Word, and a prayer. Kim knows—firsthand—that caregivers need resilience, confidence, and faith in Jesus. She winsomely delivers these in abundance.

Rev. Reed Lessing, senior pastor
St. Michael Lutheran Church, Fort Wayne, IN

Weary Joy is itself a respite for persons who care. Kim's detailed writing connects the function of the brain—in easy to understand terms—with the reality of daily human activity, shared from her own experiences in caring. Like the surprise of a laugh from a good joke, this reader found surprise after surprise: questions to help guide discussion and deeper thought; appropriate and ample use of God's Word offering forgiveness, hope, and strength; and stories that will make you laugh because at some level you will relate! I intend to use *Weary Joy* at my church for small-group study and discussion.

Rev. Dr. Kevin J. Kohnke, pastor
Trinity Lutheran Church, Walton, NE

WEARY JOY
THE CAREGIVER'S JOURNEY

KIM MARXHAUSEN

CONCORDIA PUBLISHING HOUSE · SAINT LOUIS

Concordia
Publishing House

Founded in 1869 as the publishing arm of The Lutheran
Church—Missouri Synod, Concordia Publishing House gives
all glory to God for the blessing of 150 years of opportunities
to provide resources that are faithful to the Holy Scriptures
and the Lutheran Confessions.

Published by Concordia Publishing House
3558 S. Jefferson Ave., St. Louis, MO 63118–3968
1-800-325-3040 • www.cph.org

Manufactured in the United States of America

1 2 3 4 5 6 7 8 9 10   28 27 26 25 24 23 22 21 20 19

This book is dedicated to my
husband, Paul; my son, Joel;
my daughter, Anne, and her husband, Chris.
I thank God for your care of Marx and Dorris
and their legacy.
I am thankful that we are,
for one another, a source of joy.

ACKNOWLEDGMENTS

This book would not be possible except for Reinhold "Marx" Marxhausen and his wife, Dorris (Steinbrueck) Marxhausen. Marx served Concordia University, Nebraska (Seward, Nebraska), as an art professor. He was also an internationally known artist, educator, and inventor. Dorris served the community of Seward as well as the state of Nebraska in several capacities, making good use of her interest in nature and her skills in politics. Their lives were a blessing to our family. In walking with them in their journeys of caregiving and dementia, we came to know God's gift of weary joy.

Soli Deo gloria!

TABLE OF CONTENTS

WELCOME

It seemed as if everything changed at that one particular moment. Dorris was hungry. She got in her little Smart car, the talk of her small Nebraska town, and headed for the local sandwich shop. Perhaps, as she insisted, she got her foot on the wrong pedal, or, as observers noted, she didn't slow down. Either way, she ran her car right through the front door of the restaurant. Then she got out of the car, walked into the store, and calmly ordered a sandwich.

About fourteen years earlier, my husband and I experienced a similar life-changing moment with his dad. Our families were touring Alaska after Marx spoke at a pastors conference. He kept asking where we were, and I kept updating him—Wasilla . . . Seward . . . Anchorage. It was only after about the tenth time he asked that I began to suspect he did not know we were in Alaska.

A doctor appointment following each of these incidents diagnosed them with probable Alzheimer's disease. Dorris lovingly and protectively cared for her husband for fifteen years of his eighteen-year journey with memory loss. It was less than a year after finding a memory care community for Marx that Dorris herself began to show signs of cognitive struggles.

During this time, my husband and I, living thirty miles away, raised our children, worked at our jobs, worshiped at our church, and built a life around the care that his parents needed for each stage of their illness. He started by digging his folks out of a financial mess after discovering that his mother had stopped paying bills at least seven years earlier. Together we negotiated care, ran errands, made sure that electricians and plumbers were called to do needed work, kept family updated, shopped for clothes, found in-home care, made doctor trips, kept communication lines open between doctors, refilled prescriptions, kept track of possible drug interactions, set up weekly meds, and advocated for better care. Our daughter assisted her grandparents for a time and helped to move her grandfather into a care facility, lovingly creating a space she hoped would be familiar for him. She and her brother did repair work on the property, while my husband installed a shower downstairs so Dorris could stay in the home she remembered. And for both Marx and Dorris, we remembered the sacred time of sitting, singing, and praying during hospice care.

This is a small piece of our story, of our life of caregiving. I am guessing that your story overlaps quite a bit with ours. If it does, then perhaps you agree with me that caring for loved ones is an honor that is full of what I call weary joy. It is a joy that survives weariness—a joy that doesn't come *in spite of* circumstances, but a joy *given* by our heavenly Father, which settles in and around the weariness of the task set before us. We love that person in our life who struggles with physical loss or memory loss. We grieve with our loved one, feel his or her frustration, add more work to our daily list of chores, and sigh—or cry—ourselves to sleep. Creeping out of the cracks of that grief and weariness is the joy of serving God and someone we love so dearly.

I wish I could write the book that answers the question we have all lifted up to God. I cannot explain the "why" behind our loved one's suffering. I wish I could write that elusive "how to" manual we have all searched the internet to find. No, the book God put on my heart to write is this one. I can only write a book about *our* loved ones, two beautiful children of God whose memories were called home ahead of their souls. I can tell you some of our stories, what I have learned, and what God has patiently and lovingly taught me. I pray this book can increase the joy that permeates your weariness.

This book is organized by topics focusing on issues of emotional health found in the blessings of faith. Some chapters are specific for those caring for a loved one with memory challenges, and others are for caregiving in general. Each section contains questions for family or support-group discussion and ends with a devotion tied to the chapter theme.

My prayers are with you as you walk this journey. Know that your heavenly Father deeply loves you.

> You have granted me life and steadfast love, and Your care has preserved my spirit.
>
> **JOB 10:12**

CHAPTER 1

CONNECTION:
BURDEN ON THE BRAIN

For all have sinned and fall short of the glory of God, and are justified by His grace as a gift, through the redemption that is in Christ Jesus.

ROMANS 3:23–24

For Paul and me, raising two children through the nerve-racking teen driving years was fairly uneventful. Our most memorable car accident did not involve our adolescents. It was when his mother drove through the front door of a sandwich shop.

Dorris insisted it was a minor accident. She simply hit the wrong pedal or put the car into the wrong gear, depending on which line of reasoning she was using at the time. The official police report included witness accounts that insisted she never slowed down but drove into the parking lot, over the curb, and through the front door. At that time, I was a doctoral student in the area of educational psychology, and I was taken aback by her minimization of the event. She walked through the gaping hole and went in to order a sandwich! Later, while talking with her doctor, she insisted that it was a minor accident because no one was hurt. She seemed unable to understand the potential harm. I still remember her blank stare when I insisted that someone could have been killed. It was as if her brain could not absorb this possibility.

This was not the Dorris we knew. This was not the woman who had cared for both of her parents through their dementia while raising a family three hundred miles away. She had always been able to see ahead and predict needs. Organization was a skill she dutifully shared with her community as a longtime member of the city's planning commission. Her inability to judge the seriousness of a situation was an early sign of her disease.

Dorris's inability to comprehend the implications of the accident was an example of impairment in metacognition. *Metacognition* happens when we think about what we are doing and learning. Metacognition involves preparation, thinking things through, and making needed changes in behavior. Very young children show little metacognition, although they have begun to learn it. School-age children are busy developing this skill as they learn how to get the most out of learning, listening, and completing work. While parents might insist that adolescents seem to have lost all ability to use metacognition to make right decisions, the truth is they have undergone significant brain changes and are working to adapt their metacognition to accommodate those changes.

Metacognition, at its fullest development, is what allows us to plan a project, gather the tools, and complete and assess the work. However, when we attempt something new or something that is not routine, metacognition can slip a bit. At least this is my explanation for the fact that I can count on at least three trips to the hardware store for any home project I begin. When you do something that is out of the routine, you require more brain power. This is why small changes can cause so much frustration. I cannot speak for you, but that frustration is why I hesitate to click on computer or phone updates; those "improvements" will likely upset my routine.

For an older adult, especially one battling memory loss, metacognition can be an early loss. Metacognition is a higher-order thinking skill that requires quite a bit of brain power. As the brain slows down, it can no longer support skills that allow us to apply past experiences, analyze actions, or combine important information. A connection that seems simple to us may no longer be possible for a person with reduced brain capacity. Dorris's family, friends, and the family doctor could all see that the accident was serious. Dorris could not make that connection.

But memory loss is not the only thing that can cause challenges with metacognition. For example, our brains are easily overloaded when we experience a new burden: a new diagnosis, a new loss of physical ability, and a new treatment routine are all changes that will tax mental sharpness. Most of us can improve the situation by slowing down, making lists, or sharing thinking processes with someone we trust.

FOR FURTHER DISCUSSION

1. When have you seen evidence of missing pieces of understanding from your loved one?

2. How have you been able to fill in the missing pieces?

3. When is it best to not correct and instead accept a loved one's interpretation?

GOD MAKES THE CONNECTION FOR US

This lack of metacognition also describes our state of sin. We know the laws, rules, and Commandments. We can predict the consequences of sin. We believe that God wants better for us. All of this is true—and yet we cannot stop sinning. Somewhere in this mess, there is a missing piece. We seem to be unable to make a connection between the problem of sin and preventing it.

God makes that connection for us. He does this through the redemptive work of Jesus' death and resurrection. Because of this justification, God chooses to forget our sin and counts us as righteous through our faith. Jesus is the missing piece between God and us. His work makes that connection for us. God loves us with a deep and abiding love.

As caregivers, we often supply the missing piece when words and worlds do not make sense. We explain, we remind, we ignore, and we do what is needed to help those we love who feel lost. We help them make a connection, even if it lasts only a moment. Even more, our heavenly

Father provides this care for us. Each time we fall victim to our missing pieces, each time we sin, God brings us back to Himself, wrapped in grace and forgiveness.

PRAYER

Lord Jesus Christ, I praise and thank You for Your sacrifice on my behalf. Fill me with joy in response to Your grace. Be with me as I care for our loved one, and give me the wisdom to fill in the missing pieces. Amen.

CHAPTER 2

DETACHED: RECONNECTING FOR SHARED STRENGTH

For you did not receive the spirit of slavery to fall back into fear, but you have received the Spirit of adoption as sons, by whom we cry, "Abba! Father!"

ROMANS 8:15

My work involves travel, and that means I meet many people who shuttle me back and forth between airports and conference hotels. Ron was one of those people. Sometimes the length of a ride gives us only enough time for the typical conversation about weather and travel destinations, but this ride to the airport was longer and offered more time for discussion.

Once Ron said he was a caregiver for his wife, our discussion moved in a new direction. I briefly shared my caregiving experience and asked him a question to encourage him to share whatever made him comfortable. His story was one I had heard several times before. He had to retire early from a well-paying job to be available for his wife's care. Now he was working for the hotel to make enough money to pay the bills. Here was a man who routinely asked travelers about their adventures while his life was limited to work, home, and doctors' offices. I asked him if he ever got out of the house to visit someplace or eat at a restaurant. He sighed and replied that for his wife, leaving home was just too much trouble. His world was becoming very small as he and his wife were slowly becoming separated from friends, family, and familiar activities.

Becoming a caregiver changes your world. Sometimes it changes dramatically overnight. Other times the change is so gradual that you may not realize what has happened. You drive past a favorite restaurant and can't remember how long it has been since you ate there. You look over your phone contacts list and realize that it has been months since you had a conversation that didn't involve medical information. Or perhaps someone at church asks about your hobby or hugs you to let you know you are missed at Bible study. These little messages remind you that your life is, perhaps, off-balance.

Caregiving impacts your work and other obligations. It demands time that often takes you away from work due to medical visits. It also invades your workday when chronic stress reduces your ability to focus. You no longer have time for volunteer work at your favorite charities, and busyness and weariness can prevent you from attending church and participating in your favorite group activities such as Bible study or social events.

The demands of caregiving creep into the time you spend with friends and recreation. At first, you make excuses and postpone engagements for a different time, but soon you may find that people no longer ask. Even private recreation activities become burdensome if mobility or other medical challenges present obstacles. It all seems like it is more work than relaxation.

It is easy for caregiving to borrow time from family. A house full of medical equipment often leaves little room for a family reunion. A loved one living at a care facility cannot always make the trip for holiday gatherings, and attending without your loved one can bring on feelings of guilt. Time is also stolen from immediate family members as you direct more of your resources to the one in greatest need. While the basic needs of your children and spouse are met, you may not have the time or energy for critical moments of sharing, the kinds of moments that help to build and maintain relationships.

The most significant sacrifice comes from your personal time. Everyone else, from co-workers to family members, will find a way to demand your time, but it is too easy to ignore the things you do for your personal enjoyment. These activities—things like woodworking, reading mystery novels, cooking new dishes, or creating quilts—are things that make up your personality. But there is no longer time for hobbies, and just like that, your world has become small.

The contradiction of a smaller, more limited world is that the things you have gradually reduced in your life are actually the things that can support you in your efforts of caregiving. Friends and family can help reduce your workload as well as offer emotional support with a hug, a prayer, or a listening ear. Employment can allow you to concentrate on different challenges, and the completion of a good day's work can restore your sense of accomplishment. And personal time not only brings you relaxation, but it also helps you counteract weariness and remember your joy. When we redirect all our time to meet the needs of caregiving, we make that task even more difficult because we take that time away from our own needs.

There is not much that can be done to reduce the time needed for caregiving. Doctor appointments take time. Helping your loved one get dressed, eat, or get in and out of a car takes time. Completing the tasks that keep your loved one safe, comfortable, and alive must be prioritized. Furthermore, that priority is not always easy to accomplish. When other needs call on you, it is not easy to deny the primary needs of your care receiver.

Even though friends rarely intend to separate themselves, it happens because you are no longer traveling the same path. The similarities that made interaction easy and exciting now become differences with uncertainty added in. Friends may not know what to say or how to help. They may think that asking about the details of your life is being nosy or that answering those questions might make you sad. They likely do not realize that some conversation about anything unrelated to caregiving is just what you need. Human beings often would rather do nothing than risk making a mistake.

Additionally, it is easy to ignore the impact of surprises such as visits to the emergency room, which not only take time but also take a toll, usually resulting in more procedures of care and doctor appointments. It doesn't seem worth the trouble to plan something if you might have to cancel. Combining this reality with the false assumption that caregiving is solo work is a recipe for depression.

Unfortunately, the solutions to the problems mentioned in this chapter will only give you more work to do. However, that work will pay back in more benefits than the time it takes to make them happen. Caregiver detachment causes not only depression but other physical symptoms such as weight gain, increased blood pressure, and a reduced ability to focus. You are important, and self-care is essential. Everything suggested here will improve your outlook on life and your ability to meet the challenges of caregiving (Chappell and Funk, "Social Support, Caregiving, and Aging," 355–70).

The first order of business is to remind yourself that the burden for caregiving does not rest with you alone. Your heavenly Father knows your burdens, your limits, and your needs. Your care is a part of His plan, and it is one way He provides for the needs of your loved one. You can feel confident in asking others for help. Consider some of the following options.

- **Support group:** The idea of sharing personal struggles with strangers can be disconcerting. We direct our lives toward the familiarity of friends and family. However, there is substantial benefit in interacting with people who share your experiences, joys, and frustrations. For one thing, you will not have to feel like you are a burden when you talk about your caregiving experiences. You will network with people who can give you advice and point you toward services. And you will also experience the benefit of knowing others who can help you to understand and express your feelings about the changes in your life.

- **Accountability friend:** Identify a loving, dependable friend who will commit to touching base with you once a week. Share with this friend your plans for self-care, and let this person check each week to see what you accomplished and help you make a plan for the next week. The role of this friend should have nothing to do with guilt and everything to do with encouragement. If you feel uncomfortable asking someone to help you in this way, remember that you are not asking this person to solve your problems; you need someone to be a reliable source of a few minutes each week. You will be surprised by how this will make your brain begin to look for opportunities for self-care, if for no reason other than to share with your accountability friend.

- **"Help wanted" list:** Another thing your accountability friend might help you with is creating a list of helpers. It is hard to ask for help when we think we are a nuisance or should be able to handle everything ourselves, but most people are happy to help on occasion. Create a list of several people who can help in different categories (lawn mowing, meal preparation, grocery shopping, etc.). With several people available for each task, you will not depend on any one person. While it is hard to ask for help, remind yourself that people feel good when they can help.

- **Respite care:** Respite care is available for a range of issues. Check with your health-care provider, with area agencies that assist the aging, or with your church for possible sources of respite care. Respite care will provide you with time that is free from responsibility. This time will allow you to engage in self-care and renew your energy. Some organizations offer volunteer care, and some insurance plans will pay for care.

- **Renewal:** Think, pray, and discuss with others to identify at least one activity in which you can participate that will provide you with renewal and interaction with other people. God created us to be in fellowship so we could be healthy and help one another. Look for things that allow for flexibility and interaction. Can you engage in a Bible study with a friend who won't mind if you have to reschedule from time to time? Is there a hobby group that allows you to show up when you are free? It is essential to get away, to be involved in something that redirects your thinking, and to find human interaction ("Caregiver Isolation and Loneliness," www.caregiver.org/caregiver-isolation-and-loneliness).

FOR FURTHER DISCUSSION

1. What have you given up since becoming a caregiver?

2. What are your obstacles to respite care?

3. What activities would help you feel renewed?

ADOPTED INTO GOD'S FAMILY

The verse from Romans that begins this chapter is a beautiful reminder of God's love when we feel we are slaves to our situation. A slave has no reason to feel valued, but as children of God, our heavenly Father sees us as precious. Because of this relationship, we can bring any of our cares to God in prayer. He is our loving Father, who knows us and provides for us. Such prayers are not complaints but cries for help that He hears and answers. This relationship is strong not because of us but because of God's faithfulness. It is a beautiful lopsided relationship that serves to remind us we are not alone in our burdens.

God carries out part of His plan of care for us in the people of faith who live, work, and worship with us. In more than twenty places in the Bible, we are commanded to love one another. This love includes honor (Romans 12:10), comfort (2 Corinthians 13:11), service (Galatians 5:13), and good works (Hebrews 10:24). God is telling us that when we depend on others for help, we are living within His plan for us. We may feel this creates a lopsided relationship when we are unable to return the favor, but this view is not scriptural. Before we even knew we would need help, God commanded His people to care for one another. We follow God's command both when we give and when we receive care.

PRAYER

Lord Jesus Christ, I praise You that You brought me into the family of God through my Baptism. It brings me comfort and peace to know You care for me through the love of others. Amen.

CHAPTER 3

ADVOCATE: NAVIGATING EMERGENCY CARE

Likewise the Spirit helps us in our weakness. For we do not know what to pray for as we ought, but the Spirit Himself intercedes for us with groanings too deep for words.

ROMANS 8:26

Caregiving for an older adult occasionally involves spending the better part of the day in what I call "ER limbo." On one of these occasions, Dorris's memory care community called to tell me that she had fallen. A fall always presents a risk for head injury, and a head injury could mean a blood clot. This risk, added to her resulting back pain, made a trip to the emergency room the best course of action.

For an older adult, spending the day in the ER can be arduous. Dorris had reduced vision, so magazines did not interest her. At least I did not have to worry about making small talk, as we could simply recycle the same conversation as needed. We waited to get seen, waited for a room, waited for a doctor, waited for blood tests, an EKG, and a trip to radiology. Many tests later, we found ourselves waiting again for results from the doctor. Dorris received excellent care, but the challenge of it was an hour of actual medical care spread over many hours of waiting.

This kind of day takes its toll. Dorris was comfortable except when she was moving. Her pain repeatedly caught her by surprise, adding to the stress of the unfamiliar surroundings. This produced a near constant need for reassurance. A fragile adult needs a family advocate in such situations. He or she needs someone who can fill in forms, hand over necessary medical cards, and sometimes give answers when the weary patient cannot summon the energy to repeat the story about the fall for the seventh or eighth time. Missed medications and missed meals compound these concerns.

For a person with memory loss, the ER presents even more challenges. When I accompanied Dorris's husband, Marx, to the hospital, he would sit quietly; then, every fifteen to twenty minutes, he would ask me where we were or why we were there. He went to the hospital in his small town, where everyone knew of his memory and cognition loss. Dorris, on the other hand, lived near us in a larger city, and her visits to doctors resulted in questions she could no longer answer. Even a simple request from nurses to move from an examination table to a wheelchair assumed Dorris's brain could navigate the task. This constant stress proved to make her more tired and more confused and harder to diagnose.

Elderly people with mobility challenges receive a bright yellow plastic bracelet that says "FALL RISK." Upon seeing this, hospital personnel will not expect the patient

to exit the bed alone. I don't know how many times I have wished for a similar bracelet that said "MEMORY RISK." It would have saved us much grief. Another bracelet I would advocate for is one that says "FAMILY," reminding medical personnel to make sure a family member is present when giving information.

Here is a list of things I would like every medical health practitioner to know about treating a patient with memory loss. Many of these apply to elderly patients without memory loss as well. For your convenience, these suggestions are also provided for you in the Resources section of this book (see p. 186), making it easier to share with healthcare providers.

1. Even though your patient may be able to recite his or her birth date and Social Security number, this does not mean he or she can answer your question about a fall or even current symptoms. He or she does not remember recent events and will likely give you a compilation of memories.

2. Do not ask questions of your patient while this individual is walking, climbing onto the examination table, or turning. These actions are no longer automatic and take all available cognition.

3. Please don't ask about medical history or medicine lists. Read the papers the care facility sent along, or ask the family member who is present. It might work to ask the patient to verify, but keep in mind that a memory care patient will likely say yes when the correct answer is no longer retrievable.

4. Don't ask broad or vague questions such as "Do you need anything?" Your patient will get lost trying to find an answer. Instead, ask about a specific need.

5. Do not separate a memory care patient from a loved one. This person represents all that is familiar in a stressful environment and can rephrase your questions in a way that your patient can answer. Make sure all medical information is shared in the presence of a family member.

6. While small talk can be soothing for most patients, for a memory care patient it merely adds more stress because it leaves the patient wondering if he or she knows you. Even though it feels strange, it may be a good idea to say your name, occupation, and reason for being there each time you enter the room.

Because of memory loss, our loved ones need an advocate to fill in empty spaces in memory, to anticipate challenges, and to solve problems. Those of us who walk alongside such a loved one must learn to think for two. We need to keep track of medical information and report between specialists who do not often talk to one another. We must think of the questions to ask and repeat the answers for our loved one. We often stand in their place and always put their needs first. Then, when the day has completely drained us, we must translate for other concerned family members.

FOR FURTHER DISCUSSION

1. What advice would you like to give to a medical professional about how to best care for your loved one?

2. What problems have you come across?

3. What advice would you give a fellow caregiver?

GOD ADVOCATES FOR US

In our faith life, we need an advocate. Just as Queen Esther advocated for God's people and saved them from death, we need saving. Just as Job needed someone to speak for him when his pain and grief became more than he could bear, we need such assistance. And just as Boaz stepped up and advocated as the kinsman-redeemer for Ruth and Naomi, we need a Redeemer.

When you get to the end of a long day of advocating for your loved one and wonder who advocates for you, God urges you to remember His love for you. God the Father advocates for you to provide for your needs. God the Son advocates for you, resulting in forgiveness. God the Spirit advocates for you through intercession when you are so tired you feel you can no longer pray.

God knows our burdens and loves us through our weariness. When He advocates for us, He does so in a way that anticipates our needs and anticipates our prayers. God doesn't stop there. He also advocates for us on behalf of our need for forgiveness. As you navigate these days, know that you have a wise, loving God who remembers you and the loved one you walk alongside.

PRAYER

Lord Jesus Christ, I thank You for the strength You give that allows me to advocate for my loved one when the need arises. I praise You for Your love and provision for my needs. Amen.

CHAPTER 4

SHADOW:
CARE FOR THE CAREGIVER

Keep me as the apple of Your eye; hide me in the shadow of Your wings.

PSALM 17:8

I had stopped by Dorris's house to set up her medications for the month. It was my new job after we discovered that keeping up with her medications had moved down on her priority list because of the busyness of caring for her husband. It was one of those rare warm days in January that teases us of the coming spring. When I realized that a prescription needed to be filled, I asked Dorris if she wanted to walk the four blocks to the clinic with me. I remember being surprised when she declined. My mother-in-law was a reasonably social person and an avid gardener. Because of her work in local politics, she was well known in her community. I couldn't quite comprehend her willingness to pass on fresh air and a good conversation.

This event happened before we identified her memory challenges, and some early memory loss might have been a factor. However, I suspect that one of the reasons for her willingness to pass on a walk was because she was

35

mentally and emotionally spent. Most people in her life, including her son and me, were focused on the needs of her husband. It was easy to forget the burden Dorris carried. Little by little, Dorris had given up things she enjoyed so she could preserve the energy she needed to keep her husband safe. Little by little, we found how her life had changed. Because we had not been in the home on a regular basis, we did not realize that she had begun sleeping on the living room couch so she would hear if her husband wandered out the front door during the night. She had not shared with us the changes her caregiving role brought to her life because she was practical about those changes. She did what was needed. She did not know to tell us, and we did not know to ask.

Full-time caregivers need care too. Caregivers often live in the shadow of their loved one's needs. It is not unusual for a caregiver to take early retirement or to give up a job to provide care on a 24/7 basis. A caregiver's life begins to revolve around the needs of the loved one, and there is little time left for personal needs. This takes its toll—on finances, emotions, and even physical health. The most dangerous thing about caregiver stress is that it builds slowly over time so the caregiver may not realize the degree of change or its full impact.

A chronic illness such as dementia, multiple sclerosis, or heart disease causes chronic stress for both the person diagnosed and the caregiver. Chronic stress stays under the radar, while acute stress is very evident. For example, if you are in a car accident, you experience acute stress. You can feel your heart rate rise, your hands may shake, and you might get a headache or a stomachache. Your body is telling you that you need to be alert and watch for problems. Your body makes you pay attention to the stress, but once the event is over, your stress level will decrease.

Chronic stress, on the other hand, is a relatively low level of stress that continues over an extended period. You will not feel the same level of stress as when you are in a dangerous or high-anxiety situation, but your body is aware of your stress and reacts to protect you. Chronic stress can promote a whole host of symptoms including weight gain, digestive problems, headaches, and problems sleeping or concentrating. Several of these symptoms can contribute to long-term health problems such as heart disease. Do not give in to the temptation to ignore chronic stress.

Anything you do that helps you relax will also work to reduce chronic stress. And adding even small amounts of physical activity to your daily routine will help you feel better and will work to counteract some of the harmful effects of stress ("Understanding the Stress Response: Chronic Activation of This Survival Mechanism Impairs Health," www.health.harvard.edu/staying-healthy/under standing-the-stress-response).

It is essential to spend time thinking about your health, especially considering that you are the primary source of help for your loved one needing care. In the Resources section of this book, you will find a Caregiver Health Inventory (p. 187). This inventory is a way for you to consider your stresses. It urges you to think about financial stress, changes to your physical and emotional health, and changes to your activity level. It also encourages you to consider some coping strategies that may work for you. This inventory is an excellent tool to complete with a loved one who can be asked to check on you and care for you. It is also useful information to share with your own health-care provider, who can then make suggestions specific to your needs. Take time now to read through the questions and consider how you would answer.

In the upper section of the chart, do you think you would write more in the center column than in the right-hand column? Have you abandoned the kinds of activities that have helped you with stress in the past? Do you have ideas on how to replace these activities? How do you feel about contacting the people who might be able to help you? Spending time thinking about the questions in this chart can be quite informative. It is good to be aware of these issues—but it can also be a burden. Problems uncovered by these questions need solutions, which gives you more to think about, more to worry over, and more to do.

Every caregiver needs a caregiver. Because of this, I strongly urge you to seek care for yourself. Make sure your primary care physician understands specifics about your situation. Check with your church to see what help they have to offer. Ask a family member to contact you on a regular basis for conversation and problem-solving. Find a counselor who can help you work through some of these questions. When people ask what they can do to help you, do not hesitate to ask them to check on you, handle a task (see ch. 2), or pray for your specific needs. Your health is important.

1. In what ways do caregivers live in the shadows?

2. How have others shown care for you?

3. What help do you need?

GOD CARES FOR US

Even when we live in the shadow of caregiving, God still knows we are there and that we have needs too. Psalm 17:8 asks God to keep us as "the apple of [His] eye." The apple of our eye is the pupil, and our body goes to great lengths to protect it. Any sudden movement close to the eye will make us blink, and if an object is heading toward us, we instinctively put up our hands between the object and our eyes. In this psalm, we remember that God loves us, and He desires to protect us. No matter what happens in our life, God's protective love remains.

The psalm also asks God to hide us in the shadow of His wings. However, when we apply this verse to the life of a caregiver, we should not understand it as hiding our problems away from view. That is not protection; it is, instead, a harmful act. Hiding problems might temporarily protect us from uncomfortable feelings, but in the long run, it is not beneficial for us. Just as God provides His wings for our protection, He also provides other sources of help in our lives. We should feel encouraged to seek out the help of a pastor, a friend, a doctor, or a counselor, as these are important ways that God protects our physical, emotional, and spiritual health. It is not a sign of weakness to ask for help. It is instead a sign of trusting God to provide what is needed to complete the task He sets before you. You should not feel guilty about asking for time for yourself. Rather, God blesses you with comfort, protection, and care.

PRAYER

Lord Jesus Christ, there are days when I am too tired to think, much less ask for help. Tuck me under Your wings and remind me of Your love and care. Please give me the strength and courage to ask for help from the people You send my way. Amen.

CHAPTER 5

OBSTINANCE: WORKING WITH DIFFICULT EMOTIONS

For I have the desire to do what is right, but not the ability to carry it out. For I do not do the good I want, but the evil I do not want is what I keep on doing.

ROMANS 7:18B–19

My husband and I, along with Dorris's doctor, determined that the car keys needed to be taken away. I drove to her house and began the conversation with the insistence on safety. The conversation went in circles for more than an hour. Throughout the argument, Dorris maintained that she had not killed anyone yet. But after I patiently repeated my arguments, the conversation ended, and I went home with the car keys in my pocket.

In a last show of defiance, Dorris reminded me that she had enough money to buy herself a new car.

"Good," I said, on the edge of my patience. "Look for something with heated seats because the next car I take away will become mine."

While this was a significant event, Dorris and I argued repeatedly about other things too. She wanted to be able to keep the newspapers and magazines on the floor by the couch; I wanted a safe walkway. She wanted to keep food out on the counter to nibble on all day; it made me squirm to see several days' worth of unfinished food left out. I was happy to drive to her house once a week to set up medications and clean, but I didn't want to spend the rest of the week worrying that she was injured or ill. Even when I worked hard to not treat her as a belligerent teenager, it still felt as if the daughter-in-law had become the mother. This was, of course, all complicated by the fact that memory challenges kept her from following safety guidelines that earlier in her life had been automatic. I knew my words of caution were no more effective than when Dorris let her cat out with a warning to stay out of the street.

For Dorris and me, this interplay was more of a game. She remembered doing this for her parents, and even if I was telling her something she did not want to hear, she knew my words showed how much I cared for her. She got frustrated with me, but amazingly, she never lashed out in anger.

Stepping into the role of caregiver is about more than the noticeable changes in your life. It includes significant changes in the nature of your relationship with the person for whom you provide care. The child becomes the parent, or the spouse becomes the nurse. While physical and mental realities make this change unavoidable, this does not guarantee that the hearts involved have met the challenge of the change.

We craft our identities over time, and the way we see our role in the world does not easily change. As an adolescent matures, he slips in and out of adult behaviors. Bringing an infant home gives you the name "parent," but the reality of that new role takes awhile to sink in. Then, as your child grows, your role continues to change. Seeing yourself as a caregiver is just the beginning of the process of changing your self-understanding. When your loved one adds the term "care receiver" to his or her identity, the process is one of grief. The change from being an equal care provider to the unequal relationship of care receiver involves heartache and loss. Grief causes anger and denial, and the care relationship is susceptible to both.

Denial is a curious reaction. It pushes off feelings we wish to avoid, but if used correctly, it can give us the determination to make a change. When I struggle to rise from a seat on the floor and realize that it now involves two hands and help from a friend, I might be in denial regarding the aging process. This kind of denial turns to determination and sends me to the gym to build up my core strength. Eventually I realize that I cannot deny aging, but I can delay some of its symptoms.

The unfortunate side of denial is the process that allows us to ignore the facts in front of us in favor of what we want to believe. In the story at the beginning of this chapter, Dorris was in denial regarding her reduced mental capacities. Driving is so automatic and the skills involved are so intuitive that it is easy to miss when a person no longer has the mental capacity to drive safely. When it happened to Dorris, my only recourse was to stay calm and remain firm. I admit that I heavily referred to her primary health-care provider's concerns. I feel confident that this kind of blame is something most doctors would encourage.

Coping with the denial involved in the grief of loss is one thing. Anger is another story. Anger admits to the loss and assumes someone is to blame. One of the most challenging truths about caregiving is that the person closest is often the target of the anger. As a caregiver, you are a safe and convenient target. Much as an infant in child care will save up distress until the parent returns, a care receiver may save the expressions of anger and frustration for the most relied-upon person, typically the person showing the most love and sacrifice. Unjust anger is entirely unfair, discouraging, and demoralizing. You are doing everything to help, and while you probably don't expect gratitude, you do not expect rage or resentment. This kind of anger presents you with four challenges.

Misplacement. The first challenge is to understand that the anger directed at you is not about you. This anger is about the health and independence your loved one has lost. You are merely in the path of the storm. As difficult as it is, staying calm and not participating in an argument over blame is the best response.

Blame. Caregiving situations can complicate the acceptance or denial of guilt as the blame is often misplaced. The loss of cognitive or physical abilities can cause your loved one to not only feel angry but also to direct that anger at you. Suddenly you find yourself blamed for not telling your loved one about a scheduled appointment, for example, when the truth is your loved one has forgotten your reminder. Or perhaps you are criticized for not completing a task quickly enough or not predicting a need. When you accept unfair blame, you may ease the situation for the moment, but you also might be encouraging your loved one to keep you as a target for misplaced anger. Yet, it does no good to argue about who is to blame. In situations such as this, it is best to respond with something like "We are both just doing our best in a tough situation." If these arguments occur frequently, then it is a good time to ask your pastor or a counselor to intervene.

Abandonment. The third challenge of misplaced anger is for the caregiver to avoid the feeling of abandonment. The sudden change in relationship roles likely means that you are no longer receiving the care you have previously drawn from this relationship. Adding unjust anger to your loss can be difficult to bear. Much like a parent or teacher who must bear the brunt of a child's wrath in response to news the child did not want to hear, your role is more critical than ever. Not only do you provide care and stability, but you also provide calm in response to high emotions. Speaking with your pastor or a good friend, asking these people to pray with you and for you, will do much to provide you with God's comfort and strength.

Negative emotions. The fourth challenge is to avoid getting stuck in negative emotions. *Emotional labor* is the term used when a person is in a situation that demands they swallow their feelings for the benefit of others. Emotional labor is stressful because you have to be able to respond in a way that may not feel natural. In a situation where there are emotional inequities, one person may be dealing with loss or trauma that causes him or her to respond inappropriately. Emotional labor allows for a response that brings the situation back to the point of emotional health. Nurses, police officers, and emergency medical technicians, who are all able to stay calm and bring calm to a fretful situation, are great examples of people who apply emotional labor (Grandey, "Emotion Regulation in the Workplace," 95–110).

Those who are most successful at applying emotional labor and keeping it from increasing their stress load are those who engage in *reframing*. In the act of reframing, you step away from the emotions to see the situation from several sides. Then you can understand things in a new way. Emotional reframing allows you to choose the appropriate emotional response.

When you are in the middle of a difficult emotional situation, your strength to use emotional labor comes only from the Creator of emotions. It is best if, in describing the situation, you take out personal pronouns and replace them with the name of God. Doing this helps you remember that the control over the situation is not yours. Here are some examples of reframing by remembering God:

- No matter what I try, I can't do anything right. *No matter what, God has control over the situation, and He can make it right.*

- I say it again and again, but I can't get through the denial. *God forgives again and again. His patience is endless.*

- I am so tired, and I don't know if I can do this anymore. *God is faithful. My weakness allows me to feel His strength.*

The work of reframing is made easier with input from others. Feedback from someone who understands can help you see your role and God's role in a difficult situation. God designed us to be in fellowship with one another, and this fellowship involves feedback as well as love and service. It is understandable that we avoid sharing our thinking with others because in difficult situations, the last thing we want is criticism or simplistic advice. However, our brain is good at building a wall of excuses around our wrong thinking. A new perspective can help us climb over that wall. The truth and perspective we hear from others is one reason why participating in a support group, spending time in counseling, and finding a good friend who will be honest all make a positive difference for caregivers.

There are some situations in which anger needs a different response. People who suffer from dementia or depression can display uncharacteristic anger as a part of their condition. Contacting a health-care provider for treatment options is essential. Anger that is caused by disease can become dangerous. If you are being abused physically or emotionally, you are also encouraged to seek help. Your physical and emotional safety is essential.

FOR FURTHER DISCUSSION

1. In what ways have you found yourself or your loved one in denial about your current situation?

2. How does unjust anger make you feel? How can you respond positively?

3. How can reframing an emotional situation lower your stress level?

GOD REFRAMES OUR SIN

God is infinitely patient with us. We sin again and again, and each time He reaches out to us with love, mercy, and forgiveness. We separate ourselves from Him, and He draws us back into His arms. This loving action continues from the moment of our Baptism, when we read or hear His Word, and each time we receive the Lord's Supper, until our death. For God, there is no such thing as emotional labor. He does not have to reframe His feeling for us. His love and patience are constant and faithful.

The passage from Romans reminds us that we struggle to do the right thing. We often know what is right, and even more often we cannot make the right words, behaviors, or emotions happen. We are entirely dependent on God for mercy, forgiveness, and salvation, all of which He willingly offers.

God reframes our sin. We come to Him with the mark of sin, and because of the death and resurrection of Jesus, we receive righteousness through faith. God does not have to change Himself to adapt to us. He changes *us* to make us fit to be His children.

Because God loves us, we can love. Because God is first patient with us, we have a model for how to be patient. Because Jesus sacrificed His life for us, we gain a new perspective on what sacrifice means. This knowledge brings us comfort, not because it represents an impossible standard but because we know that God understands and supports our efforts.

PRAYER

Lord Jesus Christ, my work as a caregiver can be trying at times. Remind me of Your infinite patience with me, and grant me the strength to do the work You set before me each day. Amen.

CHAPTER 6

GROWTH:
THE POSITIVE SIDES
OF CAREGIVING

More than that, we rejoice in our sufferings, knowing that suffering produces
endurance, and endurance produces character, and character produces
hope, and hope does not put us to shame, because God's love has been
poured into our hearts through the Holy Spirit who has been given to us.

ROMANS 5:3–5

The phone call was short and quick.

"Kim, this is Dorris. I don't seem to have a number to
call my folks in Blackburn."

After a moment's hesitation, I gently reminded her that
her parents had long since passed away. Her response
made me smile: "Oh, okay. I guess I don't have to be concerned with letting them know I will be a day late."

I always admired Dorris's practical side. Even though
her memories were seriously jumbled, her personality remained intact. She was able to see the bright side of a
reminder that her parents no longer lived. This ability to
reframe a situation was a skill that Dorris taught me. Every

challenge has a potential for good. More important, while we don't want to ignore problems, we are best able to solve them when we can frame them in a way that shows their blessings. Interestingly enough, this is an essential skill for people who rise to be experts in their field. They recognize that important learning happens in the midst of frustration and struggle. We develop resilience when we learn from challenges.

What if we apply the concept of the potential good of every challenge to caregiving? Caregiving does not just pose problems; it offers entire categories of problems. There are physical, relational, emotional, financial, family, spiritual, and even mental challenges that seem to lurk around every corner. Some days you want to throw up your hands and ask, "Really? What next?" It is easy to think of caregiving as one trial after another, but does caregiving also provide growth?

Study and practice are the means of learning many skills, but wisdom comes to us through a unique process. King Solomon was the only person I know of who was granted wisdom in one fell swoop. The rest of us learn wisdom after we fail. Wisdom develops when we consider our actions and see where we started down the wrong path. And we are all aware that path is easier to see when looking backward. We can entertain wisdom when trusted friends give advice, but if that advice interferes with what we want, it may go unnoticed. It seems that the emotions that come with mistakes are what it takes for wisdom to become true learning. When we feel bad for making a mistake, our brain pays closer attention to the need to change. While God created many organs in our bodies to repair themselves, He created our brains to grow as a result of our mistakes. God's goodness extends to our failures as well as our successes.

Resilience develops in much the same way as wisdom. We learn resilience in the process of struggle. It would be so easy if God, knowing that we would one day be care-givers, built resilience into our personality. Then when the time came to be resilient, we would be ready. Of course, the biggest stumbling block in this plan is that the posses-sion of personal strength would only deter us from leaning on the power of our heavenly Father. We would instead lean on our own understanding (Proverbs 3:5). The resil-ience God teaches us through the trials of caregiving is perfectly suited to help us continue to endure because this resilience comes from the lessons our brains learn at the point when they are most necessary. We learn wisdom when we fail, and we learn resilience when we flounder. That is when God teaches us what we most need.

At first glance, it does not seem to make sense that we develop resilience in struggle. When we think of resil-ient people, we think of those who are always reliable and confident. We don't stop to think about how they got to be that way. Take King David, for example: it is amazing how resilient he was while facing Goliath. He wasn't born that way; God nurtured his resilience by giving him challenges with wild animals attacking his flock of sheep. Once David saw that God was there to help him through those trials, he knew he could face the giant because God would be there too. Our fear, failure, and weariness point us toward our need to trust God.

Through David's life, we see that God does not save difficulties for people who already have the necessary skills and endurance. Nor does God simply bestow strength at the moment of necessity. Instead, God cultivates resilience as His children experience difficult times. When we grow stronger in the process of hard times, it is easier to remember that God is responsible for the change.

We should not be surprised by research that finds as many positive as negative outcomes from caregiving. We have frequent reminders that caregiving can have a negative impact on physical and emotional health. These reminders are essential because they urge us to take care of ourselves so we are healthy enough to care for our loved ones. However, it can become too easy to sit in that negative mind-set and ignore the positive side of caregiving. Growth from caregiving congregates in three main categories: faith, relationships, and emotional regulation (Hughes, "A Strengths Perspective on Caregiving at the End-of-Life," 156). Here are some of the things that research tells us are signs of growth resulting from caregiving experiences.

- **Faith:** Scripture tells us that faith grows through God's Word and Sacraments. There is no reason to believe that the trials of this life increase our faith. However, if trials remind us that we cannot cope alone and this realization sends us to His Word and His Holy Meal, then difficulties do set a stage for nurturing faith. When things are going well, it is easy to forget God's blessings and replace thoughts of gratitude with trust in our own abilities. Caregiving involves both grieving and the turmoil of each change bringing on more struggles. It is as much a lesson in receiving care as

it is an opportunity to give care. The strange benefit of this near-permanent state of neediness is the
reminder of God's love and care for us—no matter our
circumstances.

Children who always get what they demand grow up
with a strange kind of anxiety. Because they have not
learned that their parents still love them even when they
say no, they come to believe falsely that their parents love
them only when they say yes. Now their world is a scary
place because they must always be manipulating people
into following their will. On the other hand, children who
learn to survive their parents saying no develop confidence that their parents make good decisions for them
and that their parents' love is unconditional. These children do not need to manipulate others because they can
regulate their emotions with trust.

The realization that God's love is constant even in difficult situations is one way that trials and tribulations help
us to grow. In caregiving, you hear devastating news, but
each time, in your grief, you trust that God is caring for
you. When disappointing news accompanies new treatments and responsibilities, you remember God's care.
When life presents us with few problems, we too easily
come to believe that we are responsible for our success.
A day of challenges is a continual reminder of the need for
God's intervention.

Living a life of this kind of neediness not only reminds
us of our need for God, but it also reminds us of our need
for other people. It is uncomfortable to depend on others
for rides, chores, food, or other care. However, your need
becomes someone else's blessing as they serve. God

blesses us, and we are then able to share those blessings with others. If I have a car and the time to offer a ride to a doctor appointment, it is not an inconvenience for me to serve. Instead, it is a way for me to remain grateful. If I have experience with finances and wading through insurance forms, it is a blessing for me to share that gift with a fellow human being. The opportunity to share skills is the best thing about fellowship. God does not bless each of us with all of the skills, possessions, and time we will need to handle each struggle. Instead, He spreads those blessings around and gives each of us an opportunity to serve.

While it is good to feel grateful for the service of others, it is essential to remind yourself that Christian fellowship does not keep tally marks on who gives and who takes. When we serve one another, we serve God's purpose. When we receive service, we are still part of God's purpose.

- **Relationships:** Humans can be a puzzle. God created us to be in fellowship with Him and with one another. Our brains and bodies work better when we cultivate healthy relationships. Nonetheless, as we develop as humans, we strive for independence. Babies learn to walk and talk, allowing them to be less dependent on parents. Children and adolescents learn in school so they can one day support themselves and leave their parents' home. As a society, we see strength in independence, yet when God created our brains, He created a learning system that works best in collaboration with others. It is part of the human puzzle that we are strong not just because of muscles or brains but because of our relationships.

When we interact with others, when we serve someone or depend on someone, we have the opportunity to learn more about one another. These interactions also offer us the opportunity to deepen relationships as we learn to trust and accept people. How has your relationship changed with your loved one? When my mother-in-law worried that she was a burden, I had an opportunity to remind her of how much I learned from her. When my father-in-law was in memory care, my visits would be times of quiet waiting—a quiet time my busy, stressful life rarely allowed. Each interaction, whether verbal or nonverbal, was a treasure. Although it has taken time to adjust to a change in roles, to begin to care for those who cared for me as a child, it has helped me to grow because it has given me a new purpose.

Family relationships outside of the close caregiver/care receiver relationship also have the opportunity for growth. When my children provided care for their grandparents, I knew they were practicing empathy and selflessness. They also showed me strengths and skills I did not realize they had. Their acts of care cultivated confidence as they discovered what they were capable of accomplishing. I am confident they are more resilient in their lives because of their opportunity to love and serve their grandparents.

Although family relationships can strain under the burden of caregiving, they can also strengthen as members remind one another of their shared purpose. Busy lives encourage us to neglect communication, while caregiving can encourage more interaction due to the necessity of making decisions. Even stresses and arguments can result in strengthened relationships. When the needs of a family member are involved, it can be harder to ignore problems. Problems faced and solved become an added layer of strength to a family bond.

- **Emotional regulation:** Research done on the growth potential found in caregiving tends to focus on the personal growth of the caregiver. One of the most active areas of growth mentioned is that of confidence. Caregivers continually find themselves in situations that require courage and determination. When we consider the fact that we learn confidence when we survive struggle rather than when life is easy, we can see that caregivers have more opportunity than most to develop confidence. It is interesting to note that confidence developed through resilience is not necessarily confidence in *your* abilities but confidence that forces you outside of yourself; family, friends, and God will help you endure. Caregivers learn to be confident from the process of receiving help in problem-solving situations. But confidence in our abilities comes with a tinge of doubt that our talents will be able to solve every problem.

Providing care for a loved one develops a strong sense of satisfaction, which promotes skills in empathy. Much like confidence, a sense of satisfaction comes from a job well done. When we complete work that has a definite purpose, even if that work is unappreciated, we cultivate feelings of fulfillment. Caregiving also nurtures skills of empathy. To care for another person, we have to develop the ability to see things from his or her perspective. This perspective does not mean we understand how the person feels, but it helps us to imagine how *we* might feel, or what we might need, if we were in the same situation.

It is important to note that when we practice empathy, we are not practicing self-pity. Empathy not only helps us to be good caregivers, but it also helps us to rise out of our sadness, frustration, and stress. If we do not wallow in self-pity, we are better able to care for ourselves too.

The state of self-pity is not a good platform for problem-solving. A sense of satisfaction and empathy are essential components of resilience, whereas resilience has no room for self-pity. Instead of self-pity, a resilient individual will display attributes of humility. We understand that humility is not thinking highly of ourselves. However, humility is also not self-criticism. Rather, humility is not having to think about yourself and your own needs. This perspective frees us to focus on God and the work He sets before us.

When my family members reached a point in our caregiving journey where we could relate and enjoy stories of our caregiving experiences, I realized that we had also reached a state of acceptance about the diagnoses of our loved ones. We were still losing them little by little, but a new peace settled into our hearts. We enjoyed retelling stories, not out of ridicule, but as part of our shared sense of purpose. We knew these stories were a gift from God to bring us shared joy in the midst of our grief. These stories were an important part of both our memories and our grieving process.

FOR FURTHER DISCUSSION

1. How has caregiving helped you to grow?

2. How have your relationships been tested and improved?

3. In what areas would you like to continue to grow?

FORGIVENESS AND GROWTH

Without God's mercy and forgiveness, not only would we be without salvation, but we would also experience life without growth. A world that denies guilt and accepts no failure is one that promotes a mind-set of fear because there is no way to improve. God knows that we cannot follow the Law to the point of earning salvation. Jesus' death and resurrection has already won salvation on our behalf. Even though the Law does not save us, it serves other functions. It curbs our behavior, shows us our sin, and guides us toward a healthier, happier life. The Law leads us to repentance, and as God grants forgiveness, His Spirit reminds us of the benefit of the Law written in our hearts. Repentance and forgiveness allow us to grow and learn.

A child will not learn a new skill until he or she realizes the need for it. Likewise, we will not benefit from the Law until our guilt shows us the need to heed its direction. God brings good out of everything, even our sins, our weaknesses, and our failures.

PRAYER

Lord Jesus Christ, I thank You that my struggles and failures can be a source of blessing. Because of Your gifts of repentance and forgiveness, I can learn and grow in any situation. In this way, I know that You are good, all of the time. Amen.

CHAPTER 7

HIDDEN:
THE ROLE
OF IMPLICIT MEMORY

Remember Your mercy, O LORD, and Your steadfast love, for they have been from of old.

PSALM 25:6

Our daughter, Anne, was walking down the hall with her grandmother in the memory care community where she lived when they saw another resident coming toward them. Dorris turned to our daughter and said, "I'm avoiding that person. I am not sure why I am avoiding that person, but I'm sure I have my reasons."

Anne stifled a giggle and politely steered Dorris in a different direction.

We might assume that such a statement came because Dorris lacked inhibition due to her memory loss, but she was not a vindictive person by nature. There is another possible explanation: something might have triggered her *implicit memory*. Implicit memories are those that are stored and used unconsciously. For instance, once we learn to tie our shoes, we can do it automatically. We can think about other things as we effortlessly tie knots and bows.

Implicit memories are often connected to other skills. We can't learn to ride a bike without learning new aspects of balance. Because implicit memories are so well connected in our brain, they are also used to help a brain make sense of new situations. If you were to learn to ride a unicycle, your brain would rely on your implicit memory of balancing on a two-wheeled bike. It is as if we pull out an old map to journey into uncharted territory. Most of the time this works because the brain is capable of learning a new skill by creating a new map out of the old one.

Our brain typically stores implicit memories with the emotions that accompanied them. On occasion, the emotions can be triggered first; for example, the smell of cinnamon might rekindle feelings of time spent in Grandma's kitchen, and we might then recall Christmastime baking sessions. One reason the brain encodes memories with emotions is so that it has more than one way of accessing those memories. Learning skills with music is a good example. If you learn information in the form of a song, your brain can store that information along with the music and the emotions the music evokes. Now your brain has several ways to retrieve that information.

For a person with memory loss, the disease impacts different parts of the brain, and the rest of the brain has to replace the work of the damaged part, often accessing those memories in different ways. The brain can do this for a while, but eventually it can no longer compensate. The brain begins to depend on old memories and implicit memories to make sense of a new situation. I remember a similar conversation with Dorris's husband while walking with him in his memory care community. He turned to me and said, "I think this must be a women's dorm." Marx taught at a college for many years. His memories about dorms were still accessible, and because he was not able to form new memories of where he was, he used old memories to make sense of the situation.

Implicit memory can also help explain how someone with memory challenges can perform some tasks but not others. It depends on how practiced the task is and what memories can be accessed. Likewise, the emotional connection found in implicit memory can help us to understand how a loved one might be anxious about completing a task that is no longer required. Dorris had to reassure Marx so often that he had "no cows to milk" that she had a T-shirt made with those words on it.

FOR FURTHER DISCUSSION

1. When have you felt lost with your loved one?

2. What examples of implicit memory have you seen in your loved one? Have you experienced anything that you were surprised he or she could still do?

3. How do you make sense of your world, given the changes brought on by your loved one's memory loss?

GOD REMEMBERS US

Our memory systems are beautiful and intricate. The fields of neuroscience and psychology are just now creating models that help us understand how we learn and remember and how we forget. God's memory is more straightforward for us to describe. God remembers everything, and He remembers it forever. He chooses to forget our sin, but He never forgets His children.

When caring for a loved one who is fading away brain cell by brain cell, it is easy to feel forgotten. When facial recognition goes, hand-holding or back rubbing can be a new form of recognition. The memories are still there, buried beneath the disease.

Feeling forgotten is a lonely, discouraging feeling. When you care for someone with cancer or heart disease, you know your loved one will remember you. However, memory loss can leave you feeling lost in a relationship that used to be comforting. You begin to wonder if your presence matters. Please know that it does. Your Baptism made you a valued member of God's family.

Throughout this journey, I hope you remember that God's love for you and His recognition of you is constant. Just as nondamaged parts of the brain step in to keep the brain working, God steps in to provide the implicit memory of you. As you hold your loved one's hand, God is there, remembering both of you and remembering for you. He is aware of your pain, and He is mindful of your quiet joy as you experience these tender memories.

PRAYER

Lord Jesus Christ, thank You for remembering me and choosing to forget my sin. I walk in Your love and grace. Amen.

CHAPTER 8

PREPARE:
THE DECISION
TO FIND A CARE COMMUNITY

Let not your hearts be troubled. Believe in God; believe also in Me. In My Father's house are many rooms. If it were not so, would I have told you that I go to prepare a place for you? And if I go and prepare a place for you, I will come again and will take you to Myself, that where I am you may be also.

JOHN 14:1–3

Our daughter was on a mission. She made countless trips back and forth between her grandparents' home and the care community. The room her beloved grandfather was going to be living in needed to be perfect. She knew which chair was his favorite. She found the perfect table and carefully selected books for him to look through. She included drawing paper and art materials in case he wanted to communicate through creativity. She even picked out his favorite clothes because she could see her grandmother was not up to it. Anne prepared a room for her grandfather, and God blessed her work. Her father and I were very proud of her for completing this difficult task. We did not ask her to do it; she simply saw that it needed doing.

Choosing that time to move a chronically ill loved one to a care facility is never an easy task. Even the word *facility* can make us squirm. Many such places are moving away from that term and toward the descriptor *care community*. *Care community* is a better description because it is a community of people who are living and working together. But even with the idea of a community instead of a facility, few people want to leave their home, and even fewer of us want to take a loved one out of a familiar environment. As caregivers, it is easy to feel we have failed when we relinquish care to a nursing home, rehab center, assisted-living facility, or memory care community. It is a challenge even to put strong emotions aside while we think through such a decision. Please know this: if you are considering moving your loved one to a care community, you are not a bad person. Adult children and spouses sometimes have to make these decisions, and these decisions reflect love, not selfishness.

There are few clear signs to indicate it is time to seek facility care. For many, this decision is made for them when a crisis happens such as a severe fall or a new need for medical assistance. Most people who have experienced such an event would say that the best time to move is *before* a crisis, and most professionals in the field would agree. For loved ones with memory challenges, there is an added concern: the longer we wait, the more difficult it is to create a space that feels familiar and safe, and this can significantly increase agitation.

When working with the challenge of deciding on facility care, it is important to consider four areas: mobility, equipment, assistance, and discernment.

- **Mobility:** Mobility issues tend to change slowly, so it is good to take time to evaluate how a loved one and the caregiver can navigate the environment. How limited is their space to move around? Are they able to get out of the house for recreation purposes? For people with mobility issues, their environment can gradually shrink. When caring for loved ones with memory issues, mobility may create additional challenges. Can this person wander off from home and find his or her way back? What does the caregiver have to do to keep this person safe, especially at night? Caregivers need rest, and they will not get that rest if they are trying to sleep with one eye open. When considering mobility challenges, it is also important to look at the caregiver's physical strength in light of the size of the person with mobility challenges. Think seriously about the possibility of caregiver injury if the care receiver were to fall.

- **Equipment:** Those receiving care often have special equipment to assist in that care. Additionally, there are new kinds of equipment popping up on the Internet that can help with caregiving. It is essential to evaluate the equipment being used to feel confident that it is being used correctly and safely. It is also good to take inventory to see if other challenges could be resolved with the assistance of special gear. It is especially good to pay attention to medical equipment and not assume that its usage is correct and safe. At some point, a care community with access to a wide range of equipment is the best way to provide appropriate and safe assistance.

- **Assistance:** Nearly every community has in-home care providers that can assist with many different needs, from bathing to giving medications to merely providing companionship for the care recipient and the caregiver. However, even with proper care providers, the situation may reach the point that the overall care is insufficient because it is divided into little pieces. A shower aide can assist with safe weekly hygiene, but the service is of no benefit if there is a fall in the bathroom on a different day. A house cleaner who comes once or twice a week cannot make sure that walkways are safe and clear all of the time. It is a blessing to have these services available, but the care recipient's health changes continuously, so overall care still needs to be evaluated.

- **Discernment:** Even the elderly who do not suffer from cognitive decline can be vulnerable to scam phone calls, mail, or email. When my mother-in-law was caregiving, we noted that she was neglecting decisions regarding house repairs and maintenance. My husband felt his parents were safe in their home, but we soon learned they needed assistance in other areas that had not previously occurred to us. From this, we learned that it is dangerous to assume that the caregiver has everything under control. Caregiving is a huge responsibility, and care of a loved one takes priority over less urgent work. It is all too easy to focus on the needs of the care recipient and neglect the fundamental needs of the person providing care.

In the Resources section of this book, you will find a chart to use as a safety checkup (see pp. 189–90). This chart can be used as a discussion point to evaluate if facility care is needed. It is not intended to be used only once; rather, it is designed as a tool to help with ongoing evaluation. Ideally, this is something that should be done on a monthly basis with other family members, a primary health-care provider, or a social worker. It is also an excellent tool to use during a family discussion if there is disagreement regarding the need for care. It is a wonderful goal to stay in the home, but only if staying in the home is safe for both the care recipient and the caregiver.

In my father-in-law's situation, the decision to move him to facility care came because we could see that my husband's mother was no longer able to provide the necessary care. This was not an easy decision for her as she wanted to maintain his care until the end of his life. However, facility care was the best decision for each of them: Marx needed care that left Dorris in an unsafe situation. While we cannot know if he would have received better care at home, we do know she made this decision out of love.

As you continue to evaluate care options, try to keep a mind-set of possibilities. It is easy to get bogged down with the burden of day-to-day care and simply become determined to take control yourself. It is good to take time to think of potential problems and to think about the possible solutions offered. It is also best to have this discussion with extended family, friends, or professionals who can provide a perspective other than your own.

FOR FURTHER DISCUSSION

1. What are your most significant concerns for safety as you care for your loved one?

2. What services or equipment have you found that solved a problem?

3. God has placed people in your life who have the ability to help you with tough decisions. Can you identify them? Are you comfortable asking for help?

GOD PREPARES A ROOM FOR US

When our heavenly Father cares for us, His care comes from a strong mind-set of possibilities. He not only prepares a room for us for when we join Him in heaven, but He also prepares solutions for our challenges here on earth. He is a God of big ideas and small details. He is the God of salvation and the God of everyday needs. God does not make decisions for us. Instead, He offers tools and guidance. We find practical guidance in the people He puts in our lives to help us make decisions, and we find spiritual guidance in His Word.

Your needs as a caregiver are important to God. He wants what is best for you and for the loved one in your care. He will help you make good decisions, even the most difficult ones, because He is your loving Father. God's mind-set of possibilities includes every need and every solution. You can rest in His love and trust in His guidance as you navigate your days. He will never be distracted from His love for you.

PRAYER

Lord Jesus Christ, caregiving is a lonely road that no one is prepared to walk. Give me courage and trust as You walk this road with me. Amen.

CHAPTER 9

GUILT:
THE HIDDEN BURDEN
OF CAREGIVING

So that you are not lacking in any spiritual gift, as you wait for the revealing
of our Lord Jesus Christ, who will sustain you to the end, guiltless in the day
of our Lord Jesus Christ.

1 CORINTHIANS 1:7–8

Dorris and I were on our way to a doctor appointment when she asked, "Why do I feel like I should be telling you to turn here?" I replied that perhaps that was due to the many years she had given driving directions to her husband. Dorris's response caught me off guard: "Oh dear, did I overdirect him? Is he dead?"

This abrupt topic switch from driving directions to guilt left me speechless. I believe I assured her that while she did often give him directions, especially during his years with Alzheimer's, this was in no way connected to his death.

Child development experts often use the term *egocentric* when describing young children. While children are developing their understanding of the world, it makes sense that their views begin with themselves, and that determines their perspective. A young child has not yet fully developed what is called "theory of mind." This means young children do not realize that other people think their own thoughts. As the result of egocentric thinking, the child assumes that everyone knows what he or she is thinking and seeing because they must be seeing and thinking the same thing. An unfortunate consequence of egocentric thinking is the assumption that everything that happens in the world happens because of you. This is how young children can mistakenly come to believe, for example, that they are responsible for their parents' divorce. They think that it must be due to something that they did. Their perspective does not yet allow them to consider issues between their parents alone.

Adolescents can become temporarily egocentric because of brain changes that give them a very different view of their world. They might revert to egocentrism while they work to gain a new footing with their adult brain. Their egocentrism may be comforting when the world is full of changes and stress. This egocentrism is one reason parents are so tempted to accuse their teenagers of acting like children. In reality, their teenagers probably *are* thinking and acting like young children.

The elderly who suffer from memory challenges, as well as others who are consumed by their chronic illness, may also become more egocentric in their thinking. A memory challenge may lead to this kind of thinking because the brain is no longer adept at remembering the perspective of others. Egocentric thinking may also cause some to revert to assuming that they are the cause of everything that happens. Their understanding of the world and how it works becomes narrower and simpler. Egocentric thinking may be why my mother-in-law assumed that her actions caused her husband's death.

People who live with a chronic illness can also become egocentric because the stress of their illness forces them to focus on their situation to the exclusion of others' views. They may use phrases such as "You should have known!" or "Why didn't you think?" or "How could you not remember?" because they are assuming that your thoughts are the same as theirs. Such accusations are similar to those of a preschool child who insists that a classmate who happened to take the last purple crayon "did it just to make me mad—because she should have known I wanted it."

Egocentric thinking and behavior can make caregiving a challenge. It makes the usual day-to-day interactions more difficult because the care receiver is temporarily thinking like a child, while the caregiver might be assuming that he or she is thinking like an adult. Mix into this situation stress, worry, and weariness, and the results can include accusations, anger, and feelings of guilt.

The assumption of guilt is not a feeling limited to those whose brains are restricted by an egocentric viewpoint. When caregivers live with so much work, so many requirements, and so little understanding, we can easily slip into feelings of guilt. No matter how hard we work, there is always more to be done, and no matter what we have sacrificed, there are still needs to be met. It is easy to see how this state can deteriorate into feelings of guilt. Even when we seek help and receive advice, we can feel more guilt because we wonder how we will find the time and energy to try these new ideas. We develop feelings of guilt when

74

we take on the burden for everything. This is another kind of egocentric thinking: the idea that in order to be good caregivers, we have to be able to do it all.

And in those stolen moments of respite when you have the opportunity to feel full joy with friends or family, your heart may feel guilty for feeling happy while your loved one suffers. Soon you realize you are neglecting your own needs and that if you don't take care of yourself, you will be unable to care for your loved one. This personal neglect becomes one more reason to feel guilty. It's enough to put you in a state of despair.

Feelings of guilt are a form of grieving. When we feel guilty because of our sin, we are grieving the loss of the "good" person we thought we were. When we feel guilty about our caregiving, we are grieving about the "perfect" care we wish we could provide. This grief piles on top of the grief over the loss of memory or loss of health in the person for whom we care. This guilt and grief can invade our thoughts and disrupt our sleep. It doesn't seem to matter that friends and family offer thanks for the care we provide and assure us that no guilt is necessary. A caregiver can still feel guilty. When we experience guilt from so many different directions, we often end up feeling shame.

Shame is dangerous because it affects the way we think of ourselves. When we feel guilty about neglecting to do something, we can repent, be forgiven, and ask God to help us do better in the future. When we feel shame, we live in a state of mind that says there is no way to address our inadequacies. This is a destructive state of mind because it does not send us to God for repentance. Instead, it causes us to stay in a state of hopelessness. Shame is another kind of egocentrism because it says, "I am to blame, I cannot fix it, and so nothing can be done about it." God's plan for repentance and forgiveness keeps us from shame because it reminds us that the solution is outside of ourselves. The solution is God's mercy and grace lavished on us through Jesus.

FOR FURTHER DISCUSSION

1. How have people made you feel guilty about your caregiving?

2. How have you condemned yourself?

3. What does it mean to do your best?

GOD HAS A PLAN FOR OUR GUILT

We humans often have trouble understanding guilt the way God intends. The world says that guilt is unhealthy. God helps us to understand that guilt is a necessary emotion. When we sin, we should feel guilt. Guilt is part of what reminds us that we need to repent and turn to God for mercy and forgiveness. In this way it forces us to realize that our egocentrism cannot work. We need God.

Once God forgives us, guilt no longer has a purpose. We are forgiven children of God, guiltless and free to continue in His grace. What God does for us because of the sacrifice of Christ is perfect and complete.

The problem is that we seem to feel the need to hang on to that guilt. We cannot believe that we are not responsible for washing away our sin. When we don't know what to do with it, we let grief pile up in our hearts, keeping us from the joy of forgiveness. Piles of old guilt will lead us to shame, and shame can only lead us away from God.

Think about this: God knows that His forgiven children will go on to sin again. Yet He forgives us despite this. He forgives us each time we sin and repent, for as long as we live. It is an expression of His perfect love for us.

If you have guilt over how you behave, feel, or react as a caregiver, then repent and ask God to forgive you. And then confidently ask Him to take away your feelings of guilt as He loves and supports you in your daily work. It is not God's will for you to drag your guilt along with you. When we partake of the body and blood at the Lord 's Table, we walk away leaving our guilt behind. It is His will for you to live in His grace. He knows your burdens are great and that you have no strength left to carry the weight of guilt.

PRAYER

Lord Jesus Christ, I praise and thank You for Your sacrifice that brought me forgiveness. Be with me as I work. Bring me to a place of repentance when that is needed, and then allow me to let go of my feelings of guilt. Amen.

CHAPTER 10

MUSIC:
THE GIFT OF CALM

And whenever the harmful spirit from God was upon
Saul, David took the lyre and played it with his hand. So
Saul was refreshed and was well, and the harmful spirit
departed from him.

1 SAMUEL 16:23

Years ago, my husband and I made a trip to Missouri to
check on his grandmother. We stayed at her house, but after the fifth or sixth time we had to introduce ourselves, we
contacted Paul's mother and shared our concerns about
her memory challenges. The thing that was most striking
to me about that visit was how this lovely woman, who
did not seem to remember she had guests staying in her
home, could sit at her piano and perfectly play one hymn
after another. Her piano is now in our home, and when my
husband plays it, I think of her.

Paul's grandmother was for many years the organist at
her church. She likely spent many hours practicing piano
and organ. I think she spent these hours not only practicing
for performance but perhaps practicing simply because of

the joy music brought to her day. I know this is true for many of her grandchildren and great-grandchildren.

Being able to play an instrument is part of implicit memory. Because musicians practice particular procedures so often, these procedures stay as strong memories. Additionally, music is a tool the brain uses to encode memories. This means that specific events can be stored in memory along with the music that accompanied it. Because we access them together, a particular song can trigger a memory, and a memory can remind us of a piece of music. Not only that, but when we listen to music, we use many different parts of the brain. God designed our brains to make good use of music.

When I taught school, I assigned my students the task of memorizing the lyrics of the songs they would be singing for the children's Christmas service. When my students recited the stanzas, we would all chuckle at how hard it was to say the words without singing them. They would start the verse in words and usually end up in song. The words and melody were forever linked in their memory. These were their favorite memory assignments. I suspect the music created good emotions, making this memory work more pleasant.

In the Bible verse, we see an example of music as therapy. Just as the sound of the harp brought a sense of calm to King Saul, music can impact our emotions too. Music can cheer us, remind us of a sad event, get us excited, or calm us down. Music is an excellent tool for both a care receiver and a caregiver. If your loved one is struggling with memory challenges, music can be an essential tool to stimulate conversation and memories and to distract from upsetting moods. Music therapists recommend playing songs from your loved one's adolescence and young adulthood, as these are the songs that stick with us the longest. Songs of faith are also compelling, as they can rekindle church and family memories. The music might bring back specific memories, or it might bring back a mood associated with the music. You might want to consider programming your phone or computer with favorite songs to use at a moment's notice.

Because music is connected to both memories and emotions, music works equally well with those who do not suffer from memory challenges. Music can take us out of negative moods and remind us of the blessings of positive emotions. Singing in church, attending concerts, practicing an instrument, playing music in the home, and listening to private playlists on your computer or phone are all activities that can inspire a sense of peace and renewal.

If you are a musician, by all means use your gifts to entertain your loved one. Do not be concerned about a perfect performance. Your goal is to stimulate or comfort, not to amaze. If your loved one is a musician, encourage him or her to play music. Even if he or she can no longer play an instrument, just holding the instrument while listening to music can be helpful. For some, the opportunity to play with a toy instrument, buzz a kazoo, tap a tambourine, or shake a maraca can bring joy. It is a blessing from God when music either calms or sparks an interest.

FOR FURTHER DISCUSSION

1. What is your favorite music? What is the favorite music of your loved one?

2. How might you use music to stimulate or calm?

3. What hymns offer you comfort as a caregiver?

GOD BLESSES US WITH MUSIC

The great theologian Martin Luther understood the potential of God's gift of music. He tells us that Satan cannot bear the joy experienced in music (Plass, *What Luther Says*, 981). When we sing of Jesus' death and resurrection, music teaches the message of the Gospel. When we hear a song about God's love, we know and feel His mercy and grace. Music can remind us that God is with us and that we are in His care. Music can teach us about what God does for us and how He loves us. It puts God's Word into a melody, and our brains encode them together, storing them deep in our memory. Music rekindles the joy of our Baptism.

Our God is the God of salvation. He created us, watched us fall away, and sent His only Son to bring us back to Him. Our God is also the God of comfort and care. Music is an excellent example of this. We do not need music to be saved, of course, but our worship and our lives are made more vibrant because of this gift. Let the joy and wonder of music remind you of God's care.

PRAYER

Lord Jesus Christ, I praise and thank You for Your gift of music. I thank You for its ability to remind me of Your love. Help me to feel Your peace and joy in the gift of music. Amen.

CHAPTER 11

GRACE:
THE CORRECT APPLICATION

But God shows His love for us in that while we were still sinners, Christ died for us.

ROMANS 5:8

Sometime after her dementia diagnosis, Dorris's sense of balance became compromised, and her health-care professional wanted her to use a walker. Dorris was able to walk reasonably well, but she occasionally lost her balance. When she stood up to walk, she did not feel like she needed her walker, so trying to teach her to use it was a challenge for everyone in her care community.

While Dorris was not successful at remembering to use her walker, she did remember the struggle. One day, with determination in her voice, she announced, "I want my bicycle back. If I can get back to riding my bike, maybe I can convince them I don't need my walker."

"I'll see what I can do," I replied.

She ended the conversation this way: "The only good thing about this conversation is that I will have forgotten it by tomorrow."

When dementia attacks the brain, it doesn't go about lowering IQ or collectively deadening memories. Different parts of the brain are impacted, while other parts remain working. Dorris was unable to remember to use her walker, but she could remember that balance was a problem she needed to solve. She couldn't correctly apply logic (i.e., someone who needs a walker probably cannot ride a bike), but she was aware that she would likely forget our conversation.

Conditions that create memory challenges create holes in the memory process that can leave both the care receiver and the caregiver confused. It is a challenge to know what someone with memory challenges is aware of or even what time period their memories are from. In the story above, Dorris was confusing "now"—a time when she needed to use a walker—and "past"—a time when she rode her bike. This is the difference between *explicit* and *implicit memories*. Implicit memories are typically processes. Implicit memories are not usually talked about— we just do them. In fact, sometimes they are called "procedural memories." Explicit memories, on the other hand, are the memories we talk about. They are the recollections of factual information and specific episodes from our past. Dorris was using her explicit memory to make a plan regarding her bike, but she was doing this while unaware of how her implicit memory was influenced by her change in physical abilities. In other words, just because she remembered she could ride her bike, that did not mean she could actually do it. To Dorris, the request for a bike made perfect sense.

When your loved one struggles with the loss of skills due to memory challenges or the progression of other illnesses, discussions about what he or she can still do can be a challenge. Even if thinking skills are still intact, it is easy to overestimate what can be accomplished. Someone with a heart condition might think he can mow the lawn, when the very idea would make his cardiologist cringe. Another person with gradual vision loss may insist she can safely drive.

People who lose skills due to age, illness, or memory challenges grieve the loss of those skills. As caregivers, we might interpret their insistence on doing things as defiance when in fact it may be denial or lack of awareness of their loss. Those who are losing memories have the added complication of being unable to form new memories about their limitations. For Dorris, the realization that she needed to use a walker was a new memory her brain was unable to form. Every time she caught herself nearly falling, she would insist it was the first time it had happened.

In a situation that requires a person to adapt to the loss of abilities or to other changes, the caregiver's response can make all the difference. If we argue with our loved one, we will only escalate the awkwardness of the situation and perhaps cause anxiety or hurt feelings. This is true of someone in denial about a lost ability as well as someone who is unaware because of memory loss. If I had argued with Dorris about her bike, we would have gotten nowhere. When I let the issue go, she moved on to other things.

In the case of those who do not have memory challenges, the denial or the grief needs to run its course. If you argue, the denial may increase. For safety reasons, it might be best to get help to make things like lawn mowers, ladders, and car keys disappear. It is a challenge to keep your loved one safe. It is difficult to have to take on the role of a parent for your parents or your spouse. There is grief involved in this action too.

Here we are describing a classic situation of Law and grace. When we apply the Law, we are working in the area of expectations. When we know our loved one can no longer safely drive and we talk about that reality, we are dealing with unmet expectations for freedom, responsibility, and autonomy, among others. Grace is undeserved. Grace is about mercy and forgiveness and the things we do out of our love for each other. When we allow our loved one time to grieve the loss of a skill, we are applying grace.

In my conversation with Dorris about the bike, I was tempted to remind her that she was unable to walk down the hall without leaning against the wall for support, so it would be unlikely that she could navigate on a bike. This statement would have been a statement of Law. It would have been true, but it was not what Dorris needed to hear, and it would not have convinced her of her need to use the walker.

Applying grace in a situation means giving someone what they need, not necessarily what they deserve. Frequently in discussions with memory-challenged people, it is most beneficial to simply ignore the argument. In similar situations with loved ones who have lost such skills, we need to sit alongside them, hold their hand, and grieve with them. We can show grace in an unexpected reaction, such as responding to anger with calm or showing patience with frustration. This kind of grace is not the same thing as indulgence or swallowing unfair blame. Rather, it is about suppressing the urge to be right in favor of being gracious. When people are adjusting to another loss related to illness, they are already living under the Law. The gift of grace is what they need. The gift of empathy and patience is the response that will make a difference.

FOR FURTHER DISCUSSION

1. Identify a time in your life when you deserved Law but received grace.

2. Can you think of times with your loved one when the Law has worked and when the Law has not worked?

3. What do you need to do to keep your loved one safe, and who is there to help you in that process?

GOD USES BOTH LAW AND GRACE

Think of the ways God uses Law and grace in His relationship with us. He has high expectations for our behavior; He expects perfection. He has given us the Commandments and written His Law on our hearts so that we know when we have fallen short of His will. He does this not because He thinks we can achieve His expectation of perfection. He does this because He loves us and wants us to live safe, healthy lives under His guidance. He is our loving heavenly Father.

However, God did not stop at Law. He also shows us grace. He covers us with the robes of righteousness earned for us by the death and resurrection of His Son. He offers us forgiveness and brings us back to Himself each and every time we fail to meet the expectations of the Law. We could not live life without the Law, but we could not endure life without God's grace.

When God applies the Law in our life, He gives us a taste of what we deserve. Our trials, pain, and illnesses are the result of our being sinners living in a sinful world. It is what we deserve. When God forgives us, when in His mercy He sends people to love and care for us, when He provides knowledge and tools that assist us in our struggle, and when His Word reminds us of the beauty of the Gospel message, God is giving us what we need—not what we deserve. We are dearly loved.

PRAYER

Lord Jesus Christ, Your use of Law and grace in my life is a perfect example of Your love for me. Be with me and help me to know when grace is what is needed. Amen.

CHAPTER 12

CONFUSION:
UNDERSTANDING FORGETFULNESS

For God is not a God of confusion but of peace.

1 CORINTHIANS 14:33

One day at her care facility, Dorris insisted to Paul that she lived at the zoo. This belief persisted and became more detailed as the story progressed. As Dorris saw things, she belonged at the zoo, but her friend did not, and they were trying to get back to where the tour had started to get things straightened out. As it was dinnertime, Paul gently guided the pair to the dining room and was intrigued at how they both sat down in their assigned places despite claiming they had never eaten there before.

Dorris had many such stories, including insisting she was living at a library, a bowling alley, and that she worked with the custodial staff in the basement. We always found these to be interesting stories, and I suspected that they were efforts on the part of her brain to try to reconcile and understand her living situation. A life with memory challenges offers many opportunities for illogical explanations.

There are many terms that health-care providers use to identify different kinds of forgetfulness or confusion. These mental states can happen to people who do not have a dementia diagnosis. It is essential to understand the differences and the possible implications. Here are three commonly used terms, their definitions, and contexts.

- **Forgetfulness:** We use the word *forgetfulness* when we are referring to typical episodes of forgetting, such as a missed appointment or the location of car keys. These episodes by themselves do not usually point to a medical problem. They are simply a part of life. However, they can become worrisome if an individual is concerned about developing dementia. We need to remember that being forgetful is not as much a sign of a potential memory challenge diagnosis as we might think. Dementia is more typically marked by specific kinds of confusion, such as getting lost in a familiar physical setting or in a busy conversation.

  Forgetfulness often means the brain is overworked. We are more likely to become forgetful if we are working hard to learn something new. Also, if we are tired, ill, or stressed, forgetfulness can increase. For-getfulness usually indicates we have too much on the working bench of our brain, and to compensate for this "brain busyness," the brain allows some informa-tion to fade. The idea of a working bench is a model used to describe how we learn. The working bench is where we combine the new information our senses are bringing in with old information we already know. If an individual is compromised in some way—by stress or fatigue, for instance—the working bench will focus on what is essential and may forget that dentist appointment or where the dog's leash was left the last time it was used. Forgetfulness usually improves with a reduced workload, relaxing, writing things down, or developing systems such as always hanging the car keys by the door. People with dementia are forgetful, but forgetfulness itself is not necessarily an early sign of future memory challenges.

- **Disorientation:** We experience disorientation many times and for many reasons over a lifetime. Disorientation is a motivator for learning because our brain likes to be in a state of comfort, and learning is a kind of confusion that causes discomfort. If walking through a new neighborhood feels unfamiliar, the disorientation will encourage us to find landmarks and build a mental map. If learning a new concept is disorienting, our lack of mental comfort will fine-tune our attention so we can begin to make sense of the new idea. Being disoriented by a new concept is not a sign of dementia, but disorientation in more everyday situations *is* a warning sign. For example, if you are disoriented by an unfamiliar topic but solve it by going to Google for more information, then you have experienced an example of simple confusion. However, if you walk or drive in a familiar area and experience a disorientation that makes you think you do not know where you are and this feeling does not quickly dissipate, your experience is a different matter (Ghent-Fuller, *Understanding the Dementia Experience, Book I*).

Likewise, if a person who formerly enjoyed lively conversation now avoids groups of people, it may be due to feeling disoriented while trying to keep track of conversation that jumps from person to person. These kinds of disorientation will cause changes in behavior, increase anxiety, and typically become worse over time. A doctor can test for other cognitive problems. Most doctors do simple screening procedures that test for memory challenges. Such screenings can be conducted at intervals of months or even years so results can be compared to help make a diagnosis.

- **Confabulation:** Dorris's story about the zoo can best be characterized as a confabulation. In a confabulation, a situation is misinterpreted and a backstory is produced as a way of explaining it. Some confabulations do not have an outside source but are simply constructed from a mix of past experiences. The thing to remember is that the person speaking a confabulation is not consciously trying to deceive. While they are not telling the truth and their story is not factual, they are not purposely lying. A confabulation will sound fairly coherent, and the speaker will be completely convinced it is accurate. Confabulation occurs in different contexts, but it is frequently noted in people with a dementia diagnosis such as Alzheimer's disease. It can also happen during hospitalization for individuals who have not shown previous symptoms of cognition difficulties.

In some cases, a confabulation will be behavioral instead of verbal, which means the individual will want to act out the confusion. A caregiver is unlikely to persuade his or her loved one that a confabulation is untrue. It is usually best to listen and distract, as Paul did when he took his mother for a walk to the dining room (Barba and Boissé, "Temporal Consciousness and Confabulation," 95–117).

Memory challenges, caregiving, and even aging are full of moments of confusion. It is helpful to know the nature of different types of confusion, especially if it reassures you that something more serious does not lurk around the corner. If moments of confusion are becoming more frequent, it is crucial to seek medical guidance. If a primary care provider indicates there may be a developing concern, ask to be referred to a clinic that specializes in memory disorders for specific care. Information regarding memory challenges can be unsettling, but it seldom causes harm. Ignoring a possible problem, on the other hand, rarely makes it better.

FOR FURTHER DISCUSSION

1. When have you seen examples of forgetfulness, disorientation, and confabulation in your loved one? How can you tell the difference between common confusion and more serious examples of confusion?

2. When does your own forgetfulness cause you to worry about possible dementia? How do you reassure yourself?

3. What techniques do you use to deal with bouts of forgetfulness or confusion? What are the benefits of being screened for depression?

FINDING PEACE
IN THE MIDST OF CONFUSION

Caregiving can make you feel as disoriented as someone with a dementia diagnosis. When a loved one is diagnosed with any kind of chronic illness, the lives of both the
care receiver and the caregiver change forever. Life plans
change, financial situations change, and even friendships
change. It might not feel like the life you once knew, and
that can be confusing.

Our confusion is not from God. It occurs because we
are sinners living in a sinful, mixed-up, disorienting world.
We try to make good plans and do the right thing, but sin
creeps into our every day. At the end of each day, we can
only put our head in our hands and give the day up to
God.

It is not God's will for us to live in confusion. It is His will
for us to live in peace. When we read about God's peace
in the Bible, it is easy to see it in terms of a lack of conflict.
For instance, the children of Israel had peace under the
reign of Solomon because they did not experience war.
But peace is more than that. God's peace is a feeling of
completeness. It is being able to stand in the middle of
confusion and know that God has things under control. It
is the confidence that we are His children no matter what
we face in life. This peace is not something we can manufacture—it is a gift from a heavenly Father who loves us
dearly. This kind of peace is what builds resilience during
stressful situations. Resilience is not having control over a
situation; it is being able to stay calm because the situation is in God's hands. That is God's peace.

PRAYER

Lord Jesus Christ, it is not Your will for me to live in confusion. Instead, it is Your will for all of Your children to live in peace. Grant me that peace as You bring order to my life. Amen.

CHAPTER 13

CLARITY:
CONFUSION IN THE HOSPITAL

For I consider that the sufferings of this present time are not worth comparing with the glory that is to be revealed to us. For the creation waits with eager longing for the revealing of the sons of God.

ROMANS 8:18–19

Dorris was hospitalized for four days due to a urinary tract infection (UTI). I sat with her at the hospital on and off. While she had recently begun to show signs of dementia, I was taken aback by how quickly she would move back and forth between lucid conversation and a significantly muddied understanding of where she was. When she was feeling okay, we had Dorris with her stoic manner and her poignant observations. Yet an hour later, waking from a nap, in a state of agitation, barely coherent, she would insist she was there to visit her son in the room next door.

Dorris was experiencing three characteristics that are likely to cause delirium: she had a UTI, she was running a fever, and she was in an unfamiliar hospital. In addition, her sleep had been restless, possibly causing her to be sleep-deprived. We should not have been surprised by her agitation and confusion, but its severity was concerning.

Delirium is a brand of confusion that comes on suddenly and often has a temporary cause. Medication interactions and accidental overmedication can cause delirium, as can infections or a severe lack of sleep. Symptoms of delirium include shifting attention, disorientation, incoherence, and even hallucinations. Delirium is scary for both the person experiencing it and the loved ones helplessly watching.

While uncommon in younger people, delirium is experienced by up to 33 percent of those over seventy years of age. Delirium is even more likely for those who have had surgery or who are in intensive care. It is not unusual for medical professionals to dismiss symptoms of delirium due to patient age or their focus on other issues. Delirium typically clears in a matter of days, but it can continue for months. For some, it can permanently impact cognitive abilities. It is okay to speak up and ask the doctors to do something to help your loved one. When delirium is present, health-care professionals can check for dehydration, nutrition issues, infection, or complications from medicines. Correcting these issues can reduce the symptoms of delirium, bringing comfort to someone who is already ill and in an unfamiliar place.

Family members can make a difference also. Anything that reduces isolation is helpful; visits, conversation, and other forms of stimulation such as getting up from bed and walking will reduce the likelihood of delirium. It is important to make sure your loved one has hearing aids or glasses if he or she normally wears them. Even bringing familiar objects into the room will help to reduce and possibly prevent bouts of delirium (Collier, "Hospital-Induced Delirium Hits Hard," 23–24).

When a loved one is hospitalized, it is easy to focus on the primary illness to the exclusion of other things. But it is important to understand that when an individual is seriously ill, he or she does not become the disease. Your loved one is still a whole person with a variety of needs. Attending to their lack of familiarity with their surroundings as well as the need for human interaction is an integral part of health and healing.

FOR FURTHER DISCUSSION

1. What are your concerns about possible delirium episodes in your loved one?

2. How comfortable are you with asking doctors to intervene?

3. What could be done to help a hospital stay be less stressful for you and your loved one?

GOD WILL REVEAL HIMSELF TO US WITH PERFECT CLARITY

When we are in pain or in a strange place, our brain works to make sense of the situation. In the case of delirium, the brain's attempt to make sense does not clarify anything; it only makes things worse, causing fear and agitation. This is a good illustration for how we, as sinful human beings, make matters worse for ourselves when we try to understand God through human eyes.

We want God to fit a human mold. We want God to be of our making and to do our bidding. We want His actions to make sense to us. When God doesn't match our understanding, we can be angry, sad, or confused.

When we are caregivers, our lives are dominated by our worries and our weariness. It can be hard to believe that we are children of God because we may want to ask why our heavenly Father would allow this to happen. The verses from Romans urge us to remember that our sufferings of today cannot compare with the joy we will experience in heaven. Remembering this does not take away our current suffering, but it does remind us that our heartache is temporary. The verses assure us of the hope we have in Christ. We are God's creation, brought into His family through Baptism, longing to be a part of the new life in heaven that awaits us because of the sacrifice of God's Son. Even when God does not answer our prayer in the way we want Him to, even when we are confused by our life, we know we are loved by God. This is the hope that sustains our weary joy.

PRAYER

Lord Jesus Christ, You see my suffering and know my weariness. Fill my heart with Your precious hope as You grant me patience and strength. Amen.

CHAPTER 14

CHANGES:
LETTING GO OF CONTROL

Trust in the LORD with all your heart, and do not lean on your own understanding.

PROVERBS 3:5

When Dorris moved to a memory care community, we worked hard to set up her room with often-used items so her new environment would feel familiar. She had an old black couch that she practically lived on; she napped on that couch, she ate on that couch, and she read on that couch. As her world got smaller, that old black couch was where she spent her day. It was a massive thing to move, but we brought it along because we knew it was important.

A few days later, I checked in on her to see if the room felt comfortable. She looked at me and said, "Some salesman sure sold a lot of these black couches. I sleep in a different hotel every night, and there is always this same black couch in the room."

Every time I visited, I found her sitting or napping on her beloved couch, yet for several weeks she insisted that she slept in a different room every night. I suspect that while she was comfortable in the room, it did not feel familiar.

Changes have a way of making us feel both uncomfortable and unfamiliar. After a bit, we adjust to a change, and it might feel more comfortable, but it takes awhile before things feel normal again, before they feel familiar. What we seek is a type of emotional homeostasis. *Homeostasis* is the way our body works to maintain constant levels of temperature, oxygen, water, and other factors to keep our body in relatively stable condition. When all of these things are within an acceptable range, we feel comfortable. However, if one element gets out of whack, what is merely uncomfortable can become dangerous. For instance, if our body temperature rises, we may sweat more and lose fluids, which, if left untreated, can dehydrate us. We can go from uncomfortable to ill in a relatively short period of time. Homeostasis is why feeling uncomfortable can be hard to ignore; our body takes the feeling of discomfort as a warning sign.

When our mind seeks homeostasis with our emotions, it is a bit more complicated. God designed our body to be very careful about what it needs, but our brain can be easily confused. Our brain keeps us safe by signaling danger with fear or anxiety. But our brain often misunderstands a change as something that has a potential threat. Feeling anxious is not always the correct response to what is unfamiliar.

When we are caregiving for a loved one, we experience many changes. Our loved one may lose skills or capabilities. Our schedule changes as we make room for doctor or therapy appointments. Our life become overly busy as the list of chores grows ever longer. When these kinds of changes creep up on us, something as simple as going out to eat at a casual restaurant can become a formidable task. When the care we need to provide becomes more than what we can accomplish, we may need to depend on others for help. Suddenly our feeling of discomfort shifts into something more significant as we begin to fear a loss of control. Maybe we rebel and refuse the support we know we need. We misread that feeling of losing control as a need to panic. We need to remember that allowing others to step in and help does not mean we are on the path toward losing all control. God built us to develop comfort with new situations so we can successfully adapt to changes in our life.

After a lifetime of being independent, it does not feel familiar or comfortable to let others take charge of aspects of our life. It can be disconcerting to change a routine and begin to accept help with things we used to handle on our own. When these kinds of "control" changes happen, *reframing* is a helpful tool to use. Reframing allows us to cope with an uncomfortable event by putting it in a different perspective. For example, if your loved one is temporarily in a rehabilitation facility, it can easily feel like you are losing control over medical situations and daily care. Sometimes coordinating between health-care providers is a challenge, and social workers or nurses make appointments that are not convenient. This increases anxiety.

When you reframe this situation, you choose to focus on the important things over the smaller inconveniences. In reframing, you can reassure yourself that feeling discomfort is acceptable because good care will help your loved one's stay at the facility to be shorter. A short stay and a successful trip home are more important than short-term comfort. When you reframe, you do not change the situation, but you do change the way you look at it. When you change your perspective, your emotional reaction will adjust to fit.

One way to cope with the feeling of loss of control over health care is to find areas where you *can* have control. You can take control over information by creating a file for important health-care information. As a caregiver, you are frequently the connection between your loved one and the health-care system and its different providers. It can feel like providers are asking for information that they should already have, but double-checking is an important safety feature because medical history information is not always at the provider's fingertips. As a caregiver, you are the most accurate and up-to-date source of information.

A health-care information file should include copies of insurance cards, government-issued identification cards, and any advanced directives such as a living will or "Do Not Resuscitate" (DNR) documents. See the Health-Care Information Checklist in the Resources section at the end of this book for more information (p. 191). When you take on the task of organizing and maintaining health information, you will not only refresh your feelings of control, but you will also show health-care providers that you have an active role in your loved one's care. It is easy for doctors and nurses to forget how vital caregivers are to their patient's overall health. A complete health-care information file, and your insistence on asking questions and getting complete, clear answers, will make you a better caregiver and affirm your profile with doctors and nurses. Providers will be happy to add written instructions to your file, and those who provide emergency care will be grateful for the information you have collected and organized. A health-care information file can be a different kind of control when so many other things feel out of control.

When you reframe, you can remind yourself that you are not losing control, only that your control is changing. With reframing, you can teach yourself it is better to lose responsibility for some less significant things and to hold on to the important ones. Perhaps giving up time-consuming duties such as yard work, housework, or managing finances will allow you to give better hands-on care to your loved one and to yourself. These kinds of changes are not comfortable, nor are they familiar, but they can be good. It is okay to allow your loved ones to take care of you. This is not a sign of weakness but of strength. It shows you have the endurance to weather discomfort. It shows resilience to not only survive change but also to accept it as something good.

FOR FURTHER DISCUSSION

1. What changes have you and your loved one endured over the past few months?

2. How have those changes felt uncomfortable or unfamiliar?

3. How might you reframe these situations?

GOD HAS CONTROL

When the writer of Proverbs encourages us to trust in God, he adds an additional requirement: we are to refrain from leaning on our own understanding. This is not a small task. It is one thing to convince ourselves that we put our trust in our heavenly Father. Our faith tells us that He loves us and cares for our every need. Our study of the Bible assures us that God is strong enough to fight any battle we face and that He will protect and defend us. Our faith, nurtured by Word and Sacrament, makes it possible for us to trust in God.

It is the second half of that verse that causes us trouble. What does it mean to "lean on your own understanding," and why is this so hard to avoid? When we depend on our own understanding, we are saying two things: God needs our help, and we need to understand everything that is going on. In other words, we need some control over the situation.

If we are leaning on our own understanding, we are withholding some of our trust in God. We are telling Him that we are confident that He is at work in our lives, but that confidence would be stronger if things went at least a little bit our way. Trust would be much easier if we could see the whole picture, so we ask God to make His work in our lives make sense to us. We are asking God to show us *why* we can trust in Him. We spend our lives learning to take responsibility for our actions and our needs. Then God tells us to let go of the need to control that we have so persistently developed. This sense of control has helped us to keep our anxiety at bay, but now it interferes with the blessings of trust.

Professionals, friends, and family who offer help are not so much doing things for us as they are supporting us in our work. Remember Moses trying to take care of all of the tribes of Israel by himself? His father-in-law wisely advised him to create a support network (Exodus 18:13–27). We should not try to cross the wilderness of caregiving alone just to remain in control. We need to accept the support system God creates for us. We need to accept His control.

God will love and care for us even though our trust in Him is imperfect. He scoops us up in His arms and reassures us that He knows what is around the corner and that He has a plan. He tells us to let go of control so we can feel the full benefits of His love. Only God can restore us to emotional homeostasis. Only God can ease our anxiety and put our mind at rest. The control is entirely His, and He uses it for our good.

PRAYER

Lord Jesus Christ, it is too easy for me to want control over the stressful situations in my life. I want to fix things; I want things to be better; I want things to go my way. Please relieve me of the need for control and replace that need with Your love and a strong trust in You. Amen.

CHAPTER 15

FELLOWSHIP:
THE BLESSINGS OF FRIENDS

So now faith, hope, and love abide, these three; but the greatest of these is
love.

1 CORINTHIANS 13:13

I stopped at the memory care community to pick up Dorris in time for church. She greeted me with "I am so glad to see you because there have been many accusations made against me."

"Really?" I responded. "What kind of accusations?"

"There is the threat of jail."

"You are safe here. No one will send you to jail."

"Good! Lately, I have begun to think that the only things I remember are things that didn't really happen."

This exchange shows the benefits of social capital. *Social capital* is what we gain from relationship resources. We can think of it in concrete terms as the resource found in a friend who provides respite care or runs errands. We can also think of social capital in a more abstract sense as the comfort that comes from knowing that there are people who care about us and are willing to help.

Because God created us to be in fellowship, He also designed our brain to work and learn best in social settings. Infants are born recognizing the sound of their parents' voices and with a strong desire to interact and communicate with them. Each seconds-long exchange of a coo or smile between infant and parent sets the foundation of neural pathways the brain will use to learn everything else. From birth, we want to have and benefit from stable relationships. In fact, we don't merely benefit from social capital; we are unlikely to survive without it. Research tells us that one of the most damaging things we can do to another human is to put him in complete isolation. The need for interaction is so strong that we hear stories of prisoners of war developing tapping codes and putting their lives at risk to communicate with one another.

The exchange between Dorris and me is an example of how our thoughts depend on social capital. As Dorris suffered the loss of her cognitive abilities, she grew to depend on running things past me to determine if they were real or if they were a legitimate cause for worry. When we share concerns with trusted friends and they give us a better perspective or confirm that our thinking is incorrect, we can regulate our fears and anxieties. The assurance, comfort, and even the occasional teasing of a friend can help us to realize that our emotions require some measure of correction. Sharing fears and discovering we are not alone in our thinking also has a calming effect as it reminds us that we have support and understanding from other people. Without these exchanges, our anxieties would only fester and grow.

When we interact with friends, we feel valued. This perspective is essential for caregivers who often work endless hours with little or no pay, recognition, or gratitude. In the act of conversation, a friend is telling us that our thoughts, feelings, and experiences matter. Our need for social capital is so strong that we have a specific need for a sense of belonging. When a friend sympathizes with us, we know our experiences aren't outside the norm. When a friend encourages us, we feel a sense of accomplishment in what we are doing. When a friend corrects us, we may feel a slight sting, but we know we are part of a community that cares for our well-being and our role in it.

One of the most desirable gifts of social capital is having friends who help us to reframe our pain through their acts of caring. When a friend calls or sends a card, our loneliness becomes less intense. Our grief is eased just a bit by the hugs and prayers of someone who understands our pain. Our despair finds hope in the small acts of kindness such as the gift of a meal or a ride to an appointment. Because of the friends God gives us, we are better able to survive the pain that creeps into our lives. We also reframe our pain when we offer care for others. This action renews our sense of purpose and reminds us of our blessings.

These essential aspects of social capital draw a safety net under the challenging life of caregiving. Each new day and each new doctor appointment can bring another struggle or another loss. Still we know the safety net of friendship is there. This safety net helps reduce our stress because we are aware that trusted people are available to help us solve each problem that arises. Our friends live the teachings of Christ among us. They show us love and remind us of the perfect love of our Savior.

As our friends share God's love, they provide another essential function to help us feel peace. They take our words of concern and worry and rephrase them to share with us God's perspective. They remind us of relevant Bible verses. They help us to see through the stress to find how God has things under His control. They continually tell us of God's steadfast love, even when we feel weary or unlovable (Chappell and Funk, "Social Support, Caregiving, and Aging," 355–70).

FOR FURTHER DISCUSSION

1. How has a friend helped you to reframe a negative emotion?

2. What does it mean to you to be able to provide help to a friend?

3. What other aspects of social capital have you experienced?

FAITH, HOPE, AND LOVE

Social capital is not a new understanding. It is found in God's Word anytime He teaches us about the unique friendship we realize in the fellowship of believers. What does fellowship afford us? First and foremost, it is a sense of belonging. In fellowship, we belong to the family of God through the hearing of the Word and the sharing of the Sacraments. We no longer need to worry that we are alone in our suffering or trials. God brings us into something bigger than what we can design ourselves. This sense of belonging is part of our faith.

Through fellowship, we have the means of tempering our emotions. Our anger abates, our grief eases, and our struggle becomes more bearable when other believers listen, comfort, and pray with us. In these experiences we come closer to being able to accept God's perspective on and plan for our situation, even if we cannot see it. Through this empathy of friends, God gives us hope.

The acts of kindness we receive from our friends in fellowship work to help us reframe our trials into the potential for resilience. In these interactions, we can see how God is working in our lives to bless us with endurance and courage. Without fellowship to remind us that the good in our lives comes from God, we would be more likely to try to depend on ourselves. Through these acts of kindness, God gives us trust.

The world tries to break our bonds of fellowship. It distracts us from time in worship and study of God's Word. It creates shallow connections, often through social media, that fool us into thinking we are working on relationships.

Social media might help us to keep in touch, but it can also have the effect of pulling us away from the people around us. It is our faith community that offers the most effective social capital.

When we consider the blessings of fellowship, we understand a meaningful way that God shows us His love. He built the human brain to develop empathy. He created a need within us to interact with and care for one another. He showed us that the greatest thing we can do for each other is love (Plass, *What Luther Says,* 527–29).

PRAYER

Lord Jesus Christ, You have blessed me with the gift of fellowship. I thank You for friends who in the spirit of fellowship share Your help, love, and peace to walk with me on my journey. Amen.

CHAPTER 16

SHAME:
WORKING THROUGH DESPAIR

But He said to me, "My grace is sufficient for you, for My power is made perfect in weakness." Therefore I will boast all the more gladly of my weaknesses, so that the power of Christ may rest upon me.

2 CORINTHIANS 12:9

I checked my phone to find the following voicemail: "Kim, this is Dorris. I want to know if someone will be home at your house later. I want to have a conversation to get my life straightened out."

Dorris was very familiar with the progression of memory challenges. She watched this process with her parents and her husband. She knew there was a strong possibility that she would travel this path, but the onset of cognitive challenges makes the realization of what is happening confusing. She called me because she was ashamed of the mistakes she was making.

We met and talked and determined that there was no way to resolve her confusion. We realized that due to her difficulty forming new memories, we would probably have the same conversation several more times. The reality of her situation was beginning to settle in.

Each diagnosis demands some form of acceptance of the inevitable and recognition of its effect on an individual's life. The news may be the loss of physical ability, the loss of cognitive ability, the diagnosis of a terminal illness, or chronic pain. Each is devastating in its way, and each of us reacts in our own way. Some people withdraw. Others find the need to fight the life change. Some fall into depression, while others carry on with stoic acceptance. This same process is as true for the caregiver as it is for those diagnosed.

Some people seem to accept a devastating diagnosis with little trouble. Others exhibit a startling change in their personality or in how they deal with life issues. Such a change may be a healthy coping strategy or it might be an unhealthy response that warrants care. For close to fifty years, doctors have been working to describe a reaction sometimes labeled "demoralization syndrome" (Jacobsen, Maytal, and Stern, "Demoralization in Medical Practice," 139–43).

Demoralization syndrome is an extreme reaction to a devastating diagnosis and permanent loss. Its name comes from the inability to restore morale. It is not a depression that is caused by a chemical imbalance. Rather, it is a reasonable yet unhealthy reaction to life circumstances. The despair comes from the stress of the diagnosis coupled with a sense that nothing can be done to change the situation. Someone who feels such despair may react by being passive, demanding, or uncooperative. They see little hope for improvement, especially if there is a chronic loss or chronic pain. These behaviors often mask a deep feeling of shame. This shame is not a logical shame due to actual guilt but is born of helplessness. A shame that comes from the sense that you are little more than a diagnosis.

Sometimes these feelings of demoralization are accompanied by depression, but just as often they are not. While both depression and demoralization can be eased with proper therapy, depression is typically thought of as an illness, whereas demoralization can be described as a loss of resilience. A person practicing resilience will go through a difficult time by finding a way to survive and bounce back. A resilient person grows as a result of a challenge, even if there is no evidence of hope in the situation.

We might think that resilience is defined as strength, but in reality, it is more often about perspective and relationships. People who lack resilience tend to see every obstacle as nothing more than something that stands between them and happiness. The problems that arise from chronic illness will only serve to make life more miserable. Resilient people see an obstacle as a challenge that can teach or a chance to strengthen a relationship by receiving help. The perspective of resilient people puts their minds into the mode of problem-solving instead of problem *rumination*. Ruminating is a way of dwelling on your problems, and it is not helpful to the situation or your mood. Part of reframing is looking for the "what," the "how," and the "who" that bring good to a situation. What is God teaching you? How is God helping you? Who has He placed in your life that can give you help or comfort? Reframing does not get rid of the struggle, but it does help you to see it differently. Resilience blesses us with a positive attitude. This does not mean that we ignore problems or struggles, but we maintain a positive attitude about the struggle. One way to keep a positive attitude is to cultivate gratitude.

Part of gratitude is the act of saying thank you. We think of this kind of gratitude when children are taught to be polite when they have received a gift or a service. We want children to respond with appreciation even if they don't like Grandma's Christmas gift of underwear or Uncle Bill's overly enthusiastic hugs. Part of gratitude is saying thank you despite the gift. To a certain extent that applies here. It is good for us to be thankful even when we are in circumstances that cause us pain or despair. We teach children that Grandma and Uncle Bill still deserve gratitude, even if they don't get the gift thing quite right. Likewise, we know that God deserves gratitude, even if we do not understand the reason for our circumstances. We want the gift of being relieved of the burden, but even without that, we are still grateful to our heavenly Father for His love and care.

But gratitude goes beyond that act of saying thank you. It includes the realization that God still loves us even when we experience deep pain and loss. He still loves us though we feel we have no hope. Gratitude builds resilience because it reminds us of the most important truth: God loves us and His love for us is faithful.

One way to practice gratitude is to keep a journal or a list of blessings and the people who have honored your struggle with assistance. You may not have time to write thank-you notes to these people, but even listing their acts of kindness or blessings can improve your outlook. When you do find the time to thank helpers, you will be teaching people to have empathy for your situation.

Another misconception about resilient people is that they conquer adversity alone. In reality, people who demonstrate resilience cultivate relationships because the skills of others can be helpful in stressful situations. When we try to be stoic and endure our troubles alone, we are more likely to feel we can depend only on ourselves. This is dangerous thinking that often leads to shame and despair when we are unable to do the work, solve the problem, or bear the pain. When we learn to involve others in our situation, then their skills and offering of time become part of the way we can be positive and grateful in our otherwise seemingly hopeless situation. We are not stronger by doing things alone; we gain strength from accepting help and building relationships.

Relationship resilience does not mean we cultivate relationships only with those who can be of service. Instead, each relationship we nurture offers us something. Furthermore, our relationship with that person returns a benefit as well.

Think about the relationship between an older man with memory and physical challenges and a great-grandson who is barely old enough to walk and talk. The presence of this child brightens the older man's day and enriches learning for the child. Their interactions do not demand good memory or fluent speech as they communicate on different levels. The great-grandfather has undivided attention and unlimited time for the child, and the child learns much from the interaction.

God created us to be social and to live in fellowship with one another. Each relationship we experience brings some new learning to our life. This learning is true of difficult relationships as well. In fact, during times of helplessness and hopelessness, a problematic relationship can improve when each party realizes that what divided them is less important than what connects them.

FOR FURTHER DISCUSSION

1. While most of us have not experienced complete demoralization, nearly everyone feels helpless or hopeless at some point. Describe a time when you felt that way.

2. What strategies do you use to help you feel and stay resilient?

3. Which is harder: to build resilience in yourself or in the loved one in your care?

4. How do relationships impact your resilience?

TRADING IN OUR HOPELESSNESS AND SHAME

When God tells us that His grace is sufficient for us, it does not mean that He is dismissing our pain. Indeed, it says that He has taken our situation to heart to the extent that He sacrificed the life of His Son because of our need for healing. We are not alone in our suffering. God is with us, Jesus knows our pain, and the Spirit brings us comfort. It is all right to feel despair; God has a plan for us.

And it is okay to feel some amount of shame when we realize there is nothing we can do to improve our situation. Temporary shame does not mean we have become weak. It is a reminder that we have always been weak, and that God is our protector and provider. When we remember this, we have a new understanding of how God's grace is sufficient for us. He is our strength and our hope in our times of despair and in our times of joy.

The best relationship for cultivating resilience is to abide in the Word. This means going beyond learning how to apply Scripture to given situations. Abiding in the Word means doing more than using God's Word in our prayers. Abiding in God's Word is not just the act of reading and studying. It is a living, breathing relationship that echoes in our hearts when we partake of Holy Communion. When we abide in God's Word, we trust that He promises to nurture our faith. Abiding in His Word gives us a healthy perspective and a loving relationship with God and with others.

PRAYER

Lord Jesus Christ, it is not Your plan that I flounder in hopelessness and shame. Remind me that Your grace is sufficient for me, and assure me that Your death and resurrection provide eternal life with You. Cultivate my relationship with You and others that I might abide in Your love. Amen.

CHAPTER 17

DEPRESSION:
MORE THAN JUST SAD

But He said to me, "My grace is sufficient for you, for My power is made perfect in weakness." Therefore I will boast all the more gladly of my weaknesses, so that the power of Christ may rest upon me.

2 CORINTHIANS 12:9

We must have missed the early signs. Perhaps she learned to hide them. Perhaps we weren't around enough to see the changes. The signs that did tip us off were not the typical things you see in an article on "Watching for Signs of Depression." Many years into her role as caregiver, Dorris developed a new habit. We noticed that piles of mail on the dining room table were covered by bedsheets. At first it didn't seem to be a problem, since Dorris no longer entertained. She had long ago given up her basement office, and she used available space in the dining room instead. But when Paul noticed layers of bedsheets on the table, he decided to take a look. The first thing he found was a notice from the Internal Revenue Service. The piles held not only junk mail and unread correspondence but several years' worth of unpaid bills. It took untold hours of sifting through financial documents to straighten out the situation. It took very little time for us to talk to Dorris about the possibility of depression. Now, I look back and wonder how we missed the signs of her need for care.

Our situation with Dorris must be like that of so many families caring for a loved one. The focus is on the care receiver, and attention shifts away from the one who provides the bulk of the care. There seems to be little time or money for doctor visits or counseling or medication for the caregiver. Perhaps there is no family or personal history of depression, so the possibility doesn't seem likely. Or perhaps we have adopted the idea that as caregivers, we can't afford to admit that we are not coping as well as we want others to think. And we certainly don't want our loved ones to worry about us. There just does not seem to be room for the caregiver to need care. All of these realities can prevent us from seeing signs of depression in ourselves and in others.

The characteristics of depression are familiar to most of us. We may have read about them in an article or seen them in the changing behavior of a friend or loved one. The challenge of screening for depression is that individual symptoms can be part of a normal life or part of a different diagnosis. Furthermore, no one person is likely to show all the symptoms. These variables make depression easy to miss or ignore, yet we are wise to be alert to even subtle indications that something is amiss. Here are some categories that are worth attention.

- **Mood:** The most common description of depression is persistent sadness and hopelessness, but depression is more than that. A change in personality marked by uncharacteristic irritation, anger, or pessimism can also indicate depression. And although we might think of lethargy as a sign of depression, some people may show an increase in anxiety or restlessness. Others might lose interest in favorite activities or in any social situations. Still others might express feelings of guilt. Any of these moods can be normal—they may not be depression—but they are a cause for concern.

- **Cognition:** Not everyone realizes that depression can disrupt thinking processes. Depression is not just about mood; it is a condition that prevents the brain from working effectively. Depression will impact the ability to concentrate and focus, and it is likely to increase normal forgetfulness. Additionally, troubles with concentration and mood hamper decision-making capability. A slowdown in thinking can slow down physical movements, making even simple chores seem daunting. Just as a cold can make your body tired as it fights the virus, depression can overload the senses as it alters the brain.

- **Physical well-being:** The connection the brain has to every part and function of our body is evident in the symptoms of depression. Just as it is challenging to separate mood from thinking, depression also impacts physical health. Not only does depression make it more likely that physical care such as healthy eating and exercise will be ignored, but it will also affect health in other ways. People with depression might experience a disturbance in their sleep patterns, either sleeping too much or not enough. Appetite can show similar extremes of too much or too little eating. Depression can even cause unexplained pain or digestive issues. A healthy working brain is vital to nearly every aspect of our lives. These changes in health and habits bear watching.

The most serious symptom of depression is frequent thoughts of death. For a person at risk of depression, we should never dismiss comments regarding death or suicide, or any indication that their loss of life would make things better for others. Do not assume the person is expressing hopelessness only because of his or her situation. Call for help and stay with this person until professional help arrives. If this is impossible, make sure family knows, and if you think the situation is dire, consider calling the police to conduct a "well person" check.

Thoughts of death and suicide are important warning signs. Most people suffering from depression do not get to that point. However, it can be equally dangerous to assume that depression is insignificant just because it does not show itself in disturbing thoughts or comments. Depression needs medical attention. Because it looks different in each person, it can be confusing to know if you or someone you love should be seeking help. Most of the symptoms listed in the mood, cognition, and physical well-being categories above are universally experienced outside of depression. And indeed, many of us struggling under the burdens of caregiving, or suffering loss as illness or impairment progress, will experience aspects of depression throughout this period. But in determining if there is a health concern regarding depression, it is essential to consider not just the symptoms but the change, intensity, and endurance of those symptoms.

- **Change:** A change in eating or sleeping habits and emotional reactions that are out of character are worth noting. Anxiety and other unchecked emotions will cause behavior changes that seem out of place. Depression can keep a person from practicing self-regulation, causing erratic fluctuations both in emotional reactions and daily habits. If a behavior is new or out of character, then it is worth watching.

- **Intensity:** Depression can cause emotional reactions to intensify. Where you might expect sadness, hopelessness might be expressed instead. Likewise, anger can easily replace irritation, or irritation can show up in situations that previously did not cause concern. It is wise to pay attention to a change in behavior that is accompanied by emotions that are more intense than expected.

- **Endurance:** A third warning sign of depression is when emotional reactions last longer than expected. Sadness that lasts for a long time can be an indication of grief. Grief occurs for many different kinds of losses, not just death. Grief is not an indication of depression, but those who grieve might also have depression. If changes in behavior or uncharacteristically intense emotions continue for weeks rather than days, depression might be a factor. This is one way depression can sneak up on its victims. Symptoms can be easily explained by immediate circumstances, and the person experiencing them finds a new way to cope. Soon those symptoms seem to just be a part of life. This is why it can be hard for the person experiencing depression to see the need for help ("Depression [Major Depressive Disorder])," www.mayoclinic .org/diseases-conditions/depression/symptoms-causes/syc-20356007).

One study conducted with caregivers of loved ones with memory challenges found that nearly one in three caregivers reported symptoms of depression that required treatment. Caregiver depression is a concern in any caregiving situation. We probably do not know the true percentage of caregivers who suffer from depression.

While a personal or family history can make it more likely that an individual will develop depression, research shows that other factors will increase the potential too. If the caregiver is older, living with the loved one needing care, and has been giving care for an extended period, the risk for depression rises. For Dorris, the need to sleep on the couch by the front door to prevent her husband's nighttime wandering meant that her caregiving hours were 24/7. Loved ones who present challenges such as anger or aggression or who need high levels of care can also contribute to the risk factor. The physical and financial health of the caregiver should also be considered. These factors make caregiving more challenging and increase anxiety levels. Even those who are younger and do not live with the one receiving care can be at higher risk if they are part of the sandwich generation—caring for parents while raising children. Many different things can contribute to the likelihood of depression happening for someone who, under different circumstances, would not expect such a diagnosis (Covinsky et al., "Patient and Caregiver Characteristics Associated with Depression in Caregivers of Patients with Dementia," 1006–14).

One of the challenges preventing early treatment of depression is the fact that unless the person who experiences depression says something to his or her doctor, the doctor might not suspect a problem. Also it is easy for a person suffering depression to be unaware of changes, intensity, or endurance of symptoms. Depression can quickly become the "new normal." When we add these factors to social misunderstandings of depression as being a weakness of character, the chance that someone will receive care becomes even lower.

Despite these factors, we must remember that the mental and physical health of those of us who are caregivers is vital. Diagnosis and treatment of depression will do much to assure better care for your loved one and better long-term health for you. Treatment for depression does not have to take up all of your free time and finances, as new medications and treatments show much promise. Medication for depression does not stop you from feeling sad; it allows you to feel a broader range of emotions and to control your emotions without letting them control you. Receiving proper therapy for depression will allow you to get the most out of your time with your loved one, family, and friends. God gave us emotions to help us, not to harm us. Because He created us, He knows our physical, spiritual, and emotional health are all important to our overall well-being.

Caregiving is full of sorrows, frustration, satisfaction, love, and joy. If you are unable to feel these important emotions, then do not hesitate to take advantage of the tools that God has given us to treat depression. See your doctor, talk with your pastor, discuss your symptoms with a family member or friend, or talk with a counselor. A regular medical checkup for you is critical. Your primary health-care provider can screen you for depression quickly and easily. Whether or not you are diagnosed with depression, remember to eat healthy food, exercise, find ways to socialize with friends, and take time to rest. Take care of yourself so you can care for your loved one.

FOR FURTHER DISCUSSION

1. What symptoms of depression have you noticed in yourself?

2. When you are sad or anxious, what do you do that helps you feel better?

3. Is there a friend or family member who can meet with you on a regular basis?

GOD IS STRONG WHEN WE ARE WEAK

It is easy to view depression as a sign of weakness of character. We can fool ourselves into thinking we can shake off depression with a strong will. However, depression is not a character trait; it is a malfunction of the brain.

It is a weakness in the sense that like all illnesses, we are susceptible because we are sinners living in a sinful world. We cannot shake off depression any more than we can shake off sin. In fact, when we try to conquer depression on our own, we are only fooling ourselves that we need no help. In all circumstances and conditions, we are weak and in need of a Savior.

Just as God blesses us with opportunities and tools to treat depression, He is also the answer to our sin malfunction. He is strong when we are weak. Because we are weak, we need Christ to save us. In our weakness, we become stronger than we ever thought possible because Christ's power rests on us. Our weakness reminds us of our need and sends us to our Savior.

When we rest in the power of Christ, we can stop trying to do it all on our own. When we rest in the power of Christ, we open our heart and mind to see the good in every situation, the possible instead of the impossible. Depression can leave us feeling as if we have no hope. Christ is the opposite of a lack of hope because we know He already died and rose again to save us. That is all the hope we need.

Discovering his mother's depression presented my husband with years of work to untangle a financial mess. Doing this work helped him to better support his parents. Receiving treatment allowed his mother to accept the help she needed, which allowed her more time and energy to spend with her husband. God brought much good out of this situation. We felt the power of Christ rest upon us, and that made us strong when we felt weak. That is sufficient grace.

PRAYER

Lord Jesus Christ, in my sinful condition I want to be able to do everything myself. Remind me that my weaknesses are an opportunity to feel Your strength and grace. Amen.

CHAPTER 18

EMPATHY:
HELPING OTHERS
TO UNDERSTAND

O LORD, You have searched me and known me!

PSALM 139:1

Dorris and I were at the eye specialist for her periodic eye injection. I sat with her in the waiting room, looked at the line of people waiting to check in, and sighed. Behind the counter sat two people checking in clients. In front of the counter was a line of a half dozen older adults with compromised vision. Some stood there leaning on their walkers. Time after time, when they got to the window, they had to struggle with their balance to dig in a wallet or purse for insurance cards because this is yet another doctor's office that scans cards at every visit. While I am sure they have a good reason for doing this, I can't help but wonder, what happened to empathy for the patient? Dorris and I have similar struggles at this office. I am not allowed to make an appointment while the doctor finishes. I must wait until other steps are completed and make

Dorris stand and wait at the counter just so we can follow their routine.

I am in favor of an efficiently run office that provides the best care for the best price. However, policies that do not take into account the unique needs of individual patients reduce efficiency. The elderly, the disabled, and those with chronic conditions likely are a high percentage of the patient population at most clinics, yet it seems to me that they are all run as if every patient is healthy and able-bodied. Recently, I ended up in a discouraging conversation with an intake assistant at one of the clinics my mother frequents. I was trying to explain that my mother has her insurance cards with her at all times because they are in a zipper pocket under the seat of her walker. All the assistant needed to do was to note this in my mother's file. The assistant thought I was trying to argue with her about office policy. Her lack of empathy for my mother's situation kept her from hearing my advice for solving the problem. I sighed when I realized this employee would keep causing my mother stress because it was more important that everyone follow the rules than it was to give some patients a bit of extra attention.

A *lack of empathy* means a person is unable to see a situation from the perspective of another. This lack of perception encourages annoyance because the person enforcing the policy assumes the one who cannot follow it is being lazy or arbitrary or oppositional. Sometimes this is simply cluelessness, such as when I suggested to a worker at one clinic serving primarily elderly clients that they needed more designated handicapped parking. The receptionist informed me that they followed state law.

However, state law only accommodates averages. It requires empathy to see that sometimes there is a greater need. So I kept pushing my mother-in-law across the parking lot in her wheelchair.

If society has a lack of empathy for the ill and the elderly, then it has even less understanding for those of us who care for them. After all, we are not usually sick or disabled in comparison with our loved ones. I can't count the number of times, giving in to my sinful short temper, when I have thought, "That person has no idea what my life is like."

The caregiver's life revolves around the needs of another. Between insurance management, therapy, in-home care, doctors' appointments, groceries, errands, laundry, meals, yard work, cleaning, incontinence care, hand-holding, praying, and the many other acts of love that you provide, there is barely enough time, if any, to care for your needs. Not only that, but most caregivers provide this care for free, and some even sacrifice employment and their own financial future. The life and work of a caregiver would be much easier if others could have more empathy for both the physical and emotional labor of caregiving.

The skill of empathy likely begins with *mirror neurons*. Our mirror neurons fire off when we see or hear someone else experience something. The mirror neurons create the same feeling in our brain that we see on the face of the person we are watching. God blesses us with these neurons so infants can begin learning right from their birth. The work of mirror neurons is likely why one cry in a hospital nursery can set off a firestorm of infant crying. Later, when the infant lies in the lap of a parent and they exchange coos and smiles, mirror neurons let the infant know what feelings are connected to those smiles. As the child grows, mirror neurons help them to focus less on themselves and more on how their actions impact others. They may not understand why taking a toy from the hand of another child makes that child cry, but mirror neurons help them to feel the sadness of the other child. Without mirror neurons, learning would be inefficient and slow (Winerman, "The Mind's Mirror," 48).

Science is just beginning to understand the connection between mirror neurons and empathy, and it cannot explain how people are seemingly able to ignore mirror neurons and avoid empathizing with the feelings or situation of another. I suspect the answer is something they are not looking for—namely, sin. Sometimes those who need to show empathy are unable to do so because of the stress in their own lives or because they have never taken time to build a relationship with the person who needs their empathy. Sometimes those who need others to empathize with them struggle to explain the reasons behind their request or their impatience. We live in a world that discourages authentic relationship building. We deal with people via the Internet, and we seem to have forgotten how to make connections through face-to-face interactions.

Think about life two hundred years ago. Those living in a rural area might go a long time without seeing many people but would have long conversations with immediate family members. When they ventured into more populated areas, they likely cherished their interactions with new people. For those of us who remember life before the

Internet, we probably remember more conversation too. We got to know one another by spending time together. Now, with social media, instead of learning about other people, we tend to portray an image of ourselves. Instead of interacting, asking and answering questions, we determine what people hear about us. People of today portray images instead of building relationships. This portrayal works against empathy; it works against helping one another and pushes us toward depending on ourselves— which only weakens our empathy skills.

The answer to this situation is thoughtful communication. We need to make more of an effort to teach each other about ourselves, our joys and triumphs, our discouragement and our frustrations. Apparently, our mirror neurons need some stimulation.

The first step in helping people develop empathy is thinking about what another person may need to know. What assumptions are they working with, and how are those assumptions different from your situation or that of your loved one? Do they assume that standing in line is not a problem? that every patient thinks clearly? that everyday tasks like shopping and getting to the doctor's office are easy to accomplish? that you have time to accommodate their policies or requests? Think about their view of your situation, what you know to be true, and how far apart these two realities are. Now you know some things you can share with the person who is having difficulty empathizing with you. You can help him or her learn how to help you.

The next step is finding a way to patiently teach people about your situation and how they can have more empathy. If you are like me, you will have the urge to write a long letter listing all of the problems that cause you and your loved one grief. I have discovered the hard way that this does no good other than allowing me to vent. When someone who lacks empathy is overwhelmed or is truly not empathetic, it is too easy to dismiss concerns as grumpy complaints. Empathy is not learned easily or all at once. We have the capacity to learn about one another only in small amounts, and that learning needs to be repeated over time. It takes a long time for a toddler to understand how his actions impact those around him. Adult brains learn empathy slowly too, because we must connect this new learning to past experience.

If you are trying to help a friend, a relative, or someone working in a service occupation to have a better understanding of your situation, you will need to share small bits of information and work to connect the information to something already important to the listener. The most effective technique is to share empathy-based information with a spirit of gentleness. Think about using a two-part comment that leads the person to a better understanding. The first part of the comment should teach one thing about the situation; the second should offer a suggestion or leave the listener with a thinking question. Here are some examples:

- My husband is easily confused by questions. Is there a way to simplify this process?

- My mother becomes angry when I tell her she can no longer drive. How can you help me to help her understand?

- Caring for my wife takes a great deal of time and concentration. Meeting with you in the evenings is hard for me.

- My father is no longer able to make good financial decisions. I understand you will not accept my power of attorney. How else can you help me clear up this situation?

Remember that when someone does not understand your situation, they will develop empathy only through the small steps found in interaction. It does little good for us to lose patience and tell someone the obvious—that they do not understand. When we deal with someone who has the wrong idea about our life, we need to help them see our reality. This is a challenge because as caregivers, we are already burdened with large amounts of emotional labor. We have to understand the loved one we care for, and now we also have to help other people understand our situation. This burden is compounded because we are often talking with receptionists or health insurance call centers who want to help but are limited by company policy or regulations.

It does feel like the burden of understanding rests on our shoulders. This is a huge part of the weary side of weary joy. God has plans to bring good out of our labor. When our life or the life of our loved one is made difficult by someone's lack of understanding, we will react in some way. Perhaps we say something we later regret. Perhaps we fret over our frustration quietly. God knows that if we respond with gentle teaching, we leave the situation knowing we might have made a difference for the next caregiver. Other people in our lives do not have to have our experiences in order to understand. Even though they do not walk in our shoes, they can show empathy and use it to understand better what is needed.

The challenge for you as a caregiver is to add another thing to your to-do list. One thing that helps with this is to spend more time engaging in even brief interactions with other people. This interaction is good for you and for them. Seek out people at church for small conversations. Set up a regular time for phone calls with relatives who live far enough away that they are limited in their ability to help. When a stranger serving you at a store asks you how you are doing, pretend they really want to know, and tell them something about your life. Listen to others, and practice your own empathy skills.

When I started writing this book, God began to place people in my life who were also engaged in caregiving. Many of these people were strangers, and I would never have known their stories if I hadn't allowed myself the time for those short interactions. God created us to be in fellowship with one another, and this requires communication. We can learn to care about others and to teach one another about our needs. In that process, we learn about ourselves, and we learn that we are not alone in our struggles, challenges, and joys.

When my mother-in-law heard the diagnosis of Alzheimer's for her husband, she dug deep into her steely resolve and set herself for the journey ahead. Her resolve was a good use of her resilience, but the effect left her feeling that she had to handle this alone. She often made it difficult for other family members to help. It was true that we could not understand her life, but the potential for empathy and care was there because we loved her and her husband. We pleaded with her to "help us understand and let us help." Slowly she lowered the wall of self-determination; she taught us empathy and allowed us into her struggle. The benefit of this was how much we learned that we eventually used in caring for her.

FOR FURTHER DISCUSSION

1. When have you experienced a lack of empathy from others? How could you help educate the person who dismissed your situation?

2. When have you been blessed by an expression of empathy from a stranger?

3. What kind of care and concern do you need most from the people in your life?

GOD KNOWS US PERFECTLY

Jesus teaches us about empathy in several healing miracles found in Matthew 9. At the beginning of the chapter, He tells a paralyzed man to "take heart, My son" (v. 2). Jesus forgives his sins and then heals him. Several stories later, He turns to the woman who touched His robe and again says, "Take heart, daughter" (v. 22). Jesus shows us that the forgiveness of sins is the only healing we really need, but He also offers physical healing. Still, He does not stop there; He begins the healing process by providing emotional comfort. Jesus does not have to experience what we live in order to understand our challenges and needs thoroughly.

When we depend on our own skills and resources to solve our daily problems, we turn in toward ourselves. The effect of this is twofold: we lose perspective for those around us, and we wear away at our trust in God. In our life challenges and in our faith, we need to remember that God knows us perfectly and that His empathy for our situation has wisdom we lack. He knows our sins, and He knows our need. He offers us forgiveness because that is our foremost need.

Yet He does not leave things there. He comforts us and plans for our care. He sends other imperfect people into our situation to offer help. Sometimes He asks us to teach them, but it is all a part of His plan for our care. Trust God; trust the people He puts in your life. Search Scripture to know God better; experience forgiveness in the Lord's Supper; and let Him care for you in your interaction with others.

PRAYER

Lord Jesus Christ, my needs are great, and You know those needs completely. I ask You to meet the need of my sin with forgiveness and to meet my other needs through Your perfect grace. Amen.

CHAPTER 19

ANGER:
EXCHANGING ANGER
FOR PEACE

May the LORD give strength to His people! May the LORD bless His people with peace!

PSALM 29:11

It was a silly thing, really. I was at my mother's assisted-living facility, signing in at the reception desk, but when I looked up to check the time, the clock was missing. Two people were sitting at the desk in silence. They saw me looking for the clock but said nothing. They didn't even greet me. I could feel the anger welling up inside. Even as I took a deep breath and worked to regulate that emotion, I knew my reaction was out of whack. At most of my visits, I had received a friendly greeting. Why was I so angry this one time?

Perhaps it was because it was my second visit of the day, it was late, and I was tired. Perhaps it was because I was concerned about my mother after several trips to the emergency room uncovered a problem requiring expert care. Perhaps everything was coming to a head at this moment. Regardless of the reason, my anger, plain and simple, was a matter of sin. It showed my lack of trust, my need to control, and likely, my wounded pride.

When Dorris was a caregiver to her husband, she devoted all of her time and energy to keeping him healthy and occupied. She developed procedures that allowed Marx to have freedoms while also keeping him safe. She was in control. Unfortunately, her system often kept others at arm's length. I don't know if she didn't want to admit she needed help, if she was concerned that her procedures would not be followed as scrupulously, or if she was protecting her husband. The result of her system was that other people who loved him had limited access. She could keep this up only so long before the arrangement fell apart. An angry family argument around the Thanksgiving table finally broke down her defenses, and she gradually allowed others to help. A decision was made for Marx to ride the bus to spend one day a week with his sister. This arrangement allowed the two of them time together while also giving Dorris some much-needed respite.

Anger is a tricky emotion. It is one we often choose when another feeling would be more appropriate. In my situation, I needed to remind myself that I was tired—not angry. For Dorris, her anger masked her fear of giving up some control or perhaps her sadness over the unwelcome changes in her life brought by her husband's memory challenges. We like to think our anger is justified, but it rarely is. If there is a real threat or a genuine hurt, then anger is appropriate as long as its expression is productive. Anger can motivate us to approach an offender and show him or her the need for repentance. Anger can push us to make a difference in a bad situation.

But my anger with the reception staff at the assisted-living center was not justified. They did nothing to hurt me. They just didn't meet my need in that moment. Anger is a natural emotion to fall into, and we often use it to ignore more complicated feelings. If I am angry at another person, I can blame them for the situation. However, if my anger is due to other emotions such as weariness or frustration, then the solution to the problem probably rests with me. Sometimes anger is just easier. For example, it is easier to be angry than to admit to jealousy. Blaming someone else when I don't get what I want is much easier than figuring out how I contributed to my situation or how I need to change my behavior or attitude. Anger is also easier to fall into when depressed. Again, depression requires me to do something, but anger lets me lash out or wallow in self-pity.

For caregivers burdened with grief, worries, and extra work, an occasional short temper is understandable. I repented of my anger, and I trust that God has forgiven me. Because of this forgiveness, I can forgive myself and, with God's help, try to do better. However, the temptation to give in to my anger is always there. If I give in to anger, it can become chronic. Chronic anger does not look like ranting and raving; it is more of a simmering anger. Chronic anger will morph into a miserable disposition, criticism, hostility, a lack of patience, and possibly depression. Chronic anger is corrosive; it is harmful to your physical health, your relationship health, and your emotional health. When we simmer in anger, we indulge in rumination. Rumination is what happens when we "sit" in emotion and spend too much time thinking about it. We soon find that negative emotions taint our outlook on life. We remember the bad things and forget the blessings, which only feeds our rumination. Sin creates an ugly circle, doesn't it?

It is a challenge to regulate anger. Once anger begins, the body supplements the emotion with an increased heart rate fueled by adrenalin. Recognizing the beginning of anger provides an opportunity to take a deep breath and say a prayer. Anger comes from deep in the brain, so it is also helpful to engage the thinking part of the brain by reciting a Bible verse. It doesn't have to be a verse about anger. A favorite verse that brings you comfort and peace will work. It also helps to distract your brain from the emotions of anger. See the Resources section of this book for some suggestions ("Bible Passages for Comfort and Peace," pp. 192–94).

You can also engage the thinking part of the brain by asking yourself what feelings might be hidden by the anger. It might be an emotion triggered by the event (humiliation, frustration), or it might be an unrelated cause (tiredness, lack of patience). Once you identify the hidden emotion, you can begin to redirect or reassess:

- I am more tired than usual today. I need to walk away from this and try to get to bed early.

- Her comments make me feel like I am not doing a good job at caregiving. She probably didn't mean to make me feel that way. How can I explain this?

- My patience is shot. I need people to read my mind and help me. How can I communicate my needs instead?

- This happens nearly every time I call the insurance company! I am frustrated, but that doesn't mean I need to be angry. Maybe I can try calling again later.

- I want to have control over the problems and the busyness of my life. Lord, help me hand control over to You.

I find that when my life stress is at its peak, I need to be diligent in self-care. Healthy meals, sleep, and exercise work wonders to help regulate strong emotions. I have also learned to watch for my triggers—tiredness and anxiety. This realization can help me to stay calm and prevent anger. When I have a bad day, I try to be careful not to use absolutes in my speech or thinking. Words such as *always* and *never*, especially when they come after the word *you*, are rarely accurate and lead thinking down a path toward anger.

Chronic anger can be both a contributing cause of and a symptom of depression. If you find you are frequently angry or overreact to stress, then discussing it with your primary health-care provider is a good idea. A therapist will give you techniques for self-care and help you to see events from a different perspective. Caregiving is already hard on your health. There is no need to add to it with chronic anger. A therapist will not judge you. A therapist will help you sort through things and see the solution ("Controlling Anger before It Controls You," www.apa.org/topics/anger/control.aspx).

FOR FURTHER DISCUSSION

1. What are your triggers for anger?

2. What enables you to calm down?

3. What happens when you ruminate in anger?

GOD CHANGES ANGER TO PEACE

Anger is harmful to your physical and relational health, but it is detrimental to your spiritual health as well. It is not that our anger turns God away. God is bigger than our anger, and His love for us is faithful. The harm in anger is more about what it does to us. It turns us in on ourselves, so we think only of our hurt and pain. It leads us to put our trust in our own abilities instead of leaving situations in God's hands.

This is why the psalmist tells us, "Refrain from anger, and forsake wrath! Fret not yourself; it tends only to evil" (Psalm 37:8). Look at the excellent advice from God found in this verse:

- "Refrain from anger"—find alternatives to anger.
- "Fret not"—don't allow yourself to ruminate in anger.
- "It tends only to evil"—there are negative consequences to chronic anger.

This verse is more than a therapy session on anger management. It is a reminder that God understands our lives and our emotions. He has a plan to help us.

God uses faith to turn our anger into peace. This chapter began with a verse from a different psalm: "May the LORD give strength to His people! May the LORD bless His people with peace!" (Psalm 29:11). God knows we need His strength and His peace. His strength helps us to navigate those long, tiring, frustrating, worrisome days that are all too familiar in the life of a caregiver. We want to think we are in charge of being strong, but we are just fooling ourselves. Resilience is not about having control; it is about being calm because we know God has control. Any strength we have comes from God. God is a never-ending source of strength.

God's love is patient. He is ready to take our anger and exchange it for His peace.

PRAYER

Lord Jesus Christ, I am tired and frustrated and impatient, and this puts me at risk for anger. Forgive me and fill me with Your strength that I may know Your peace. Amen.

CHAPTER 20

HUMOR:
CULTIVATING JOY

But the fruit of the Spirit is love, joy, peace, patience, kindness, goodness, faithfulness, gentleness, self-control; against such things there is no law.

GALATIANS 5:22–23

Memory and cognition challenges did not seem to impact my mother-in-law's sense of humor. After a string of mis-placed observations, she announced, "I am getting used to being wrong."

I responded, "Are you now?"

She retorted, "I know you find it hard to believe that Dorris would ever admit she was wrong without going down bloody."

This made us laugh. It was funny because we were both grieving over her level of confusion and we needed a laugh. It was funny because it was classic Dorris, and she knew it. It was funny because we both got the joke, and it solidified our bond. This quick moment of laughter completely changed our moods. It was a gift from God for sure.

Humor brings us joy, but it does so much more. When Dorris and I laughed together over her statement, we were reminded at a deep level of the love we had for each other. This reminder of love is the best way to combat loneliness. The memory of that laughter registers in a way that reminds us we are part of the broader human experience. In the world of caregiving, we have accomplished something powerful anytime we can lessen loneliness.

It is likely that you have heard that laughter can lower blood pressure and support the immune system. Did you realize it can reduce pain, anxiety, and depression? Laughing does not cure these problems, but it does reduce their impact on our lives while it boosts energy. Because we know that humor is a part of God's creative design of mankind, we should not be surprised that it acts like a wonder drug (Wilkins and Eisenbraun, "Humor Theories and the Physiological Benefits of Laughter," 349–54).

Humor fits nicely into caregiving, and not just because caregivers need to laugh. The release of tension is the basic building block of humor. A good joke makes us laugh because it strings us along, creating a bit of tension as we try to predict the punch line. We laugh when the punch line catches us by surprise. We laugh because of the incongruity or the unexpected.

Caregiving is full of the unexpected. We go to a doctor appointment and hope for good news but hear something different. We call the insurance company trying to solve a problem and end up with two more. We follow a daily routine that has worked for our loved one in the past, but a new wrinkle causes the routine to fall apart. Nearly every day we find the unexpected, and that creates tension.

Ask anyone who has survived a challenge by laughing—the bigger the tension, the heartier the laugh. We laugh to keep ourselves from crying. We laugh to survive. We laugh to find joy once again.

God gave us many different emotions. We understand that emotions make our life more memorable, and they can motivate us to do big things. Emotions are more than accents that intensify our life. Emotions are strongly connected to our cognition. They are a part of our thinking, problem-solving, and our ability to remember. Emotions change the way we think. When we are experiencing negative emotions, we have reduced ability to understand new things or solve problems. When we experience positive emotions, we not only think better, but we also build stronger relationships with other people. These strong relationships come back to increase our positive emotions. Humor moves us from a negative emotion to a positive one by forcing us to use the thinking part of our brain.

Humor requires abstract thinking. You have to comprehend what is said or done while also thinking of what makes it funny. While your brain is busy thinking about the humor, it forgets to manufacture the negative emotion. For example, we often label a pun as low humor, probably because it makes us groan as much as laugh. However, to understand a pun, you have to know the real meaning of the word as well as the intended humorous meaning. The point is anytime our brains are busy figuring something out, they have less capacity to make us feel sad or angry or stressed. This process is how laughter releases the tension caused by negative emotions.

Positive emotions are an essential part of resilience because they increase our ability to problem-solve and to endure. The challenging thing about positive emotions is that we do not consider the fact that we need to cultivate them. Imagine you are walking for several miles into a strong wind. Every inch of that mile, you will notice the force of the wind working against you. However, if you turn around and walk back, you will likely notice the help of the wind only for a short while. Soon you will take the wind for granted. That is the way we are with emotions. Negative emotions make a stronger impact on our mood, and positive emotions are often taken for granted. When we cultivate positive emotions, we are acknowledging that we have God's care and support—even in difficult times (Davidai and Gilovich, "The Headwinds/Tailwinds Asymmetry," 835–51).

Humor also helps us to reframe a situation. We can look at a challenge and see only the obstacle it presents. Or we can look at a challenge and see the potential it offers. Caregiving presents many challenges that have insurmountable obstacles. The good side of this is that caregiving continually reminds us that we need God's help. The bad side of challenges is that we may stay focused on the negative. Humor reframes the situation, bringing us joy. When we look at challenges through the eyes of joy, we see those challenges in a different, less intimidating way. We can laugh in the face of grief because we have a powerful God.

Perhaps one of the best examples of reframing a situation with laughter comes from disciplining young children. Children have to learn rules, but they get tired of hearing nothing but rules. Sometimes this causes them to dig in their heels and refuse to obey. A smart parent will not give in to rule breaking but will change the mood with humor. "What? You refuse to put your clothes in the laundry basket? Oh no! Now they won't get washed, and you will run out of clothes. I guess you will have to wear Daddy's socks and underwear." The idea of a young child wearing adult underwear is enough to make even the most contrary child giggle. Instantly, tension is released when that happens, obedience is more likely, and the child learns the reason for the rule. Humor doesn't solve the problem, but it gives us a different perspective.

How can you bring more laughter into your life? There are movie subscription services that provide funny films. The library has books, and if you are selective, the Internet offers much humor. The two best sources for laughter are friends and family. Look for ways that you can increase contact with people who know you and make you laugh. If you cannot meet in person, look into computer and phone apps that let you converse face-to-face. Human interaction is good, and laughter makes it better. These interactions will provide you with good memories to laugh over too (Fredrickson, *Love 2.0: Creating Happiness and Health in Moments of Connection*).

When I help my mother write notes to her sisters and friends, we usually go for good memories from childhood or shared times. She enjoys relating the stories to me, I enjoy hearing them, and when we send them as a note to a friend, they bring joy to still another person. These kinds of memories are great for loved ones with memory challenges as well. Joyful memories of the past tend to rekindle other memories. Think about collecting these stories into a laugh scrapbook. The stories do not have to include every detail. A short version will trigger the memory. Perhaps family members would be able to contribute to the scrapbook.

FOR FURTHER DISCUSSION

1. What makes you laugh? What makes your loved one laugh?

2. Describe how you feel after a good laugh.

3. What would you include in a laugh scrapbook?

A LIFE LED BY THE SPIRIT

The Galatians verses at the beginning of this chapter list the fruit of the Spirit. These are not characteristics that make us acceptable to God. Instead, they are characteristics that result from a life led by the Spirit; they are blessings that flow from our God-given faith.

We can choose to walk away from these blessings. We can choose to be mean instead of kind, or gruff instead of gentle. However, we realize that these characteristics make our life better and are worth cultivating. We cannot make ourselves kind or gentle, but through the power of the Holy Spirit, we can be these things. It is interesting to consider that we work toward each of the listed characteristics with the exceptions of peace and joy. It is as if we expect those two to happen on their own, and when they don't, we continue in sadness and strife.

God wants us to feel joy, and He makes it possible. The joy He gives us comes through faith, trust, and hope. The faith He gives us is our connection to Him, our reminder that He created us and sent His Son to save us. The trust He gives us is the source of our peace, our reminder that He is in control of our lives. The hope He gives us is the source of our joy, our reminder that salvation is ours. There can be no better source of optimism than God.

PRAYER

Lord Jesus Christ, thank You for joy and laughter. They remind me that You care about every aspect of my life. Bless me with a positive outlook on the challenges I find in my life, and let me be a source of joy for others. Amen.

CHAPTER 21

SHOULD:
THE DESTRUCTIVE
NATURE OF CRITICISM

Brothers, if anyone is caught in any transgression, you who are spiritual should restore him in a spirit of gentleness. Keep watch on yourself, lest you too be tempted. Bear one another's burdens, and so fulfill the law of Christ.

GALATIANS 6:1–2

I've seen the posts on social media, and I have had similar conversations while holding the hand of a crying friend. Families are a beautiful thing when they pull together, but their power to hurt is robust when criticism abounds. Our family was never openly criticized regarding our decisions for Paul's parents. If aunts, uncles, cousins, siblings, or friends disapproved of our care for Paul's parents, we never heard it. At the same time, if we had been ignoring critical problems, I hope we would have been willing to listen to concerns offered in a spirit of gentleness because this is a meaningful way we bear each other's burdens.

Many families find a way to share the jobs involved in caregiving. One person handles finances; another attends doctor visits. One person takes care of the lawn,

156

and another cleans the house. It is a blessing when tasks can be divided. However, the reality for many is that the bulk of the load falls on one set of shoulders. Often the person who bears most of the work responsibility is also in the best position to make decisions regarding care. This person is the one who sees the daily needs and knows his or her capacity to meet those needs. No one gives perfect care. Each caregiver makes some good decisions and some poor ones. When caregivers make poor decisions, they often come out of a spirit of genuine concern. Non-caregivers need to be willing to help, need to recognize that it is not always clear if a decision is right or wrong. They need to be sure their input is supporting the work of the caregiver.

Caregivers need to seek counsel from others regarding the level of care and other decisions. We also need to be assured that no one is our prophet, sent to tell us what to do. For all those involved, God is our guide. When we work together in a spirit of support, remembering that the person needing care is more important than our ego, then we have a better chance of knowing God's will.

One unhealthy mind-set is to flounder in the "shoulds":

- I should give more time to caring.
- She should keep the house cleaned.
- I should have more patience.
- He should be able to live at home.
- She shouldn't take the doctor's word for it.
- He shouldn't shut us out.
- I should visit more often.

- I should have a say in the decision.

Such statements are not helpful. They do not build relationships. They do not produce good care. They do not seek God's guidance. Some are about demands made without empathy, and others are about misplaced guilt. When we sin, we feel appropriate guilt, and that guilt leads us to repentance. The forgiveness of our sin leaves us with an opportunity to do better with the help of God.

Wrongful guilt leads only to shame or contempt. We feel shame if we know of no way to appease the guilt. No caregiver can please everyone. We feel contempt if we have criticized and felt our concerns go unanswered. We can see how the "shoulds" lead us away from God and His wisdom. It is not that the statements above are wrong; perhaps they indicate a necessary change that needs to be made. But the statements wrongly assume the speaker knows the right choice. It is hard to follow God's will when we walk our path without His guidance.

Our emotions are gifts from God. They give us the necessary motivation in situations that require us to act or react. For example, if we did not have the emotion of fear or disgust, we would likely do something that would injure or sicken us. Sometimes our emotions lead us astray. They take over our thinking. Then our brains scramble to create reasons for the runaway emotions. "I feel guilty, so there must be something I did wrong." This scenario can lead to misplaced guilt, guilt not earned.

The other option is for the brain to fight the emotion and replace it with another. "I feel guilty, but I am a good person who did nothing wrong, so someone else must be to blame." Now the guilt turns to anger, and the brain must find someone to be the target of the anger. That target is likely to be the person doing the work. This scenario can lead to misdirected guilt, guilt redirected at another person.

When the "should" statements are directed inward, the speaker may be feeling guilt at being unable to perform perfect, universally pleasing caregiving. While all caregiving can improve, no caregiver is perfect. When we strive in vain for perfection, we lose focus on the loved one needing care.

When we direct the "shoulds" at someone else, we ignore our personal guilt. It may be easier to be angry at the caregiver than to admit you feel guilty about being unable to give more help. If your "shoulds" point to a real error and lead to improvement in caregiving, then they are helpful. If not, they need to be dismissed as what they are—misplaced or misdirected guilt.

When dealing with unhelpful emotions, it is good to look at the reasons behind them. In the case of the "should" statements listed earlier, the most likely reasons are detachment and perfectionism. Recognizing the cause might result in identifying a step toward a resolution.

In this instance, we can consider *detachment* as the opposite of empathy. In empathy, we know some details about another person's situation that allow us to develop a better perspective. In detachment, those details are unknown or perhaps unused. It may not be that a person is detached because he or she refuses to empathize; it may be more of an issue of distance and a lack of priority.

Whatever the reason for the lack of empathy, detachment is not helpful in a family caregiving situation.

Detachment comes from neglected relationships. We neglect relationships when we do not communicate or look for ways to care for one another. A neglected relationship results in a weak bond. A weak family bond becomes noticeable when struggles present challenges. Just as it is easy to ignore a relationship, it is also easy to forget that a weak relationship is a cause. We fall into criticism and accusing each other of being overcontrolling or uncaring. Additionally, the sense of detachment promotes assumptions. If we don't know the details of what is happening, it is easy to assume that all is fine or that we somehow know what is best.

Keeping family relationships strong is essential, and it is hard work. We depend a great deal on our relationship with others, and Satan sees the opportunity to hurt us by weakening these relationships. He doesn't even have to introduce a struggle. He accomplishes the same result by encouraging us to feel too busy, too tired, or too frustrated to reach out and work on our connection.

Here are some general suggestions that might help to address the problems of detachment:

- **Communicate as much information as possible.** Share the frustrations, the worries, and the joys. More information promotes more empathy and reduces detachment. Consider a regular time to meet or talk. This practice helps your brain to "save up" things that need to be asked or communicated.

- **Ask for help.** A family member who lives far away likely cannot take over day-to-day tasks, but he or she might be able to help financially. Regular phone calls to the loved one needing care are a great way to offer assistance. You may have to ask more than once, as it can take awhile to replace detachment with empathy.

- **Find a mediator.** Your pastor, a mutually trusted relative, a counselor, doctor, or social worker can step in to help the decision-making process or help with a broken relationship. A knowledgeable third person rarely fixes a problem but can keep a discussion focused toward good care decisions and away from runaway emotions. In this process, a relationship can be repaired and strengthened.

- **Come together in prayer.** When we pray, we refocus our thoughts on God and away from our perspective. When we pray with the person causing us grief, the relationship moves to a state of repair. If praying together is not an option, consider communicating regular specific prayer needs. This method is a way to share more details that will be less likely to lead to defensiveness. Prayer promotes empathy, develops a shared sense of purpose, and refocuses personal desires to that of seeking God's guidance.

Perfectionism is another reason behind "should" statements. It is natural for us to try to take control of a situation to find solutions. Of course, the problem with diving into a problem is that we start to believe we must be in control. This control tends to shut out others who could help. When we insist on the burden of control, we set ourselves up for anxiety and guilt. Anxiety can cause us to freeze, making it difficult to make decisions on our own or with others. Taking control in this way moves us from relying on God to relying on ourselves. The only possible result of self-reliance is guilt because we are unable to meet the standard of perfection.

Here are some general suggestions that might help to address the problems of perfectionism:

- **Let go of control.** The care you provide will not be perfect, but it will reflect love.

- **Let others into the process.** The care others offer will not be perfect either. Learn to see the help of others as a blessing instead of a cause for worry.

- **Find support.** A good friend who is willing to offer a listening ear is a blessing. When you share your struggles, feedback from a trusted friend can help you to get control of misplaced emotions.

- **Accept God's forgiveness** when you have not done the right thing or have not done enough. Forgiveness opens the door to growth.

When you are feeling anxious, criticized, or shut out, go to God in prayer to ask Him to bless you with trust. God will remind you that when He is in control, you do not have to have all the right answers.

FOR FURTHER DISCUSSION

1. What are the "shoulds" that haunt you?

2. What might be the reasons behind them?

3. What do you need to concentrate on to be able to respond appropriately to your "shoulds"?

FROM "SHOULD" TO "WILL"

The Bible verses at the beginning of this chapter contain the word *should*. In these verses, God directs us to confront sin with a spirit of gentleness. A spirit of gentleness puts ego aside and focuses on what needs to change. Note that in these verses this confrontation is a three-step process of restoration, self-examination, and bearing one another's burdens. When we seek to restore our relationships with one another, we must be mindful of our sin and realize that the emotions of pain, guilt, anxiety, and anger can be burdens that cause us to sin.

God did not put us here to reach some self-imagined potential. God did not put us here to satisfy others with our actions and decisions. God did not put us here to please Him. He asks us to do the work He sets before us each day. He knows it will lack perfection. He knows some actions will be wrong and that our whole day will be steeped in the sin in which we were conceived. He understands this and loves and forgives us anyway.

He asks us to do the work and to trust that Jesus covers the mistakes, brings good out of the error, fills in the gaps in our abilities, and sustains us through Word and Sacrament. He asks us to love and serve one another. We serve; Jesus saves.

PRAYER

Lord Jesus Christ, my life is full of mistakes and guilt. I know I cannot be perfect, but I also know that You cover me with Your righteousness. Help me to see my need for restoration, and replace my guilt anxiety with forgiveness and trust. Amen.

CHAPTER 22

VALIDATION:
CORRECTING MISPERCEPTIONS

Out of my distress I called on the LORD; the LORD answered me and set me free.

PSALM 118:5

Dorris, my husband's aunt, and I were eating lunch and engaging in the usual small talk. Without warning, Dorris looked at us over her glasses and asked, "Are we all aware that I was shot at in the bathroom this morning?"

Slightly taken aback, we reassured Dorris that no, she was not shot at, and that she was safe.

She responded, "I wasn't? Well, it sure makes for a good story."

This conversation reminded me of when a nurse told us that Dorris was upset with a resident who kept wandering into her room thinking it was his. Dorris marched up to the nurse's station and asked them to call her son because she wanted him to bring her a gun. I imagine the nurse responded with "I'll get right on that, Dorris."

Each of these stories is an example of a kind of response known as *validation therapy*. Naomi Feil first identified validation therapy in the 1980s (Feil, *The Validation Breakthrough*). Feil was an administrator in a care center and noticed that when a resident was confused, if she used logic to try to convince the resident of his or her error, the result would be an argument. She found that for residents, especially those in a high emotional state, it worked better to refrain from arguing and replace correction with other techniques to calm and reassure.

The challenge in using validation therapy is to allow your loved one to assert something that is not true and instead focus on dealing with the emotion behind it. Some common misperceptions include the following:

- A deceased family member is still alive.

- There is a thief in the house.

- There is some sort of danger.

- This is the wrong house.

- No meals have been served all day.

- Hygiene is unnecessary.

- You are not welcome as a caregiver.

It is easy to see how these misperceptions could deteriorate into endless arguments. For instance, you could find ten ways to prove that you and your loved one are in the right home, but if lost or scrambled memories dictate the right house is the one from childhood, even your canceled check for the payment of real estate taxes will be useless. Emotions rarely bend to proof.

In responding with validation therapy, the caregiver does not address the misperception. Instead, the emotion that accompanies the misperception becomes the central issue. In the chart below, we consider the previously mentioned misperceptions and speculate on the emotion behind them.

MISPERCEPTION	EMOTIONAL CAUSE
A deceased parent is alive.	People are hard to recognize.
There is a thief in the house.	Anxiety over being unable to find things.
There is some sort of danger.	Fear due to confusion.
This is the wrong house.	I feel unsafe.
No meals have been served all day.	Confusion over body messages.
Hygiene is unnecessary	The steps for taking a shower are no longer remembered.
You are not welcome as a caregiver.	Frustration over the current situation; someone must be to blame.

In each case, the brain is trying to make sense of a senseless situation with the emotions and memories that are still available. In applying validation therapy, the goal is to reframe or distract from the misperception because while the details of the misperception can be argued about, identifying the correct emotion will likely ring true. This strategy can engage the loved one in a discussion that can help to calm the situation.

Here are some suggested responses. These examples are not intended to be a script but rather to give you an idea of how to reframe the situation using the emotional cause.

Misperception	Emotional Cause	Suggested Response
A deceased parent is alive.	People are hard to recognize.	What do you remember about your father? How did he show his love for you?
There is a thief in the house.	Anxiety over being unable to find things.	I get so frustrated when I can't find things I need. I like it when someone helps me search.
There is some sort of danger.	Fear due to confusion.	What do you do when you are afraid? What scared you as a child?
This is the wrong house.	I feel unsafe.	What is your happiest memory of your home? What looks familiar in this home?
No meals have been served all day.	Confusion over body messages.	Is your body telling you that you need a snack?
Hygiene is unnecessary.	The steps for taking a shower are no longer remembered.	What is your favorite shirt to wear? Let's find it and set it out for after your shower.
You are not welcome as a caregiver.	Frustration over the current situation; someone must be to blame.	I love you, and somedays I am frustrated and scared too.

While it is a challenge to ignore the incorrect perception or to ignore insults aimed at you because you are a safe target, addressing the emotion is likely the most effective strategy. And even if you can correct the misperception, the emotional needs are still present. A good analogy for this situation might be a small child who falls and gets a small scrape on the knee. The resulting tears are not as much due to pain from the injury as they are to fear that the sidewalk seemingly came up to slap the child in the knee, or that the pain, once started, will not abate. The reassurance that pain dissipates and that falls happen are things a child learns from experience. A bandage and a hug do not address the wound so much as they tend to the feelings caused by the fall. With validation therapy you are not validating the misperception; you are validating the emotions.

When we examine the suggested responses, we can see the use of two primary techniques: *redirection* and *reassurance*. Many of the questions access memories connected to the misperception. This strategy is a distraction technique that avoids argument while gently pointing the loved one in the right direction. For instance, if a confused individual is sure a deceased relative is alive, then the brain is using accessible memories to try to explain a feeling of anxiety. In this instance, it is likely that questions about that deceased relative help to encourage more analytical thinking. Discussion of memories might help to calm the anxiety.

Reassurance techniques focus more on addressing the disturbing emotion. These responses acknowledge the emotion and offer comfort and support. Pointing out what you suspect is the emotional cause may be ineffective. For instance, if you respond with "I know you are worried," you might find yourself in the middle of the very argument you were trying to avoid. Instead, your response can find a way to take the emotion into account ("It is worrisome when we can't find what we need") to calm the emotion with a suggested action ("Let's look together") or to admit you feel that way on occasion.

Research on validation therapy indicates it is not entirely successful. Its success likely depends on the intensity of the emotional state and the memory capacity of your loved one. It should also be noted that validation therapy does not cure anything; it is a strategy for calming emotions. However, there is no indication that using this technique is in any way emotionally harmful when used as a strategy to avoid argument (Heerema and Chaves, "Using Validation Therapy for People with Dementia").

When loved ones are confused and insisting on the truth of something that is obviously false, the safest response is one of grace, even though the temptation is to use Law and correct. A person who is confused or anxious, angry, or afraid has different needs than someone who purposely lies. In these situations, the Law does not work, as it intensifies argument rather than bringing clarity. Here, grace comes in the form of identifying and redirecting the emotions to the truth of God's love and care.

FOR FURTHER DISCUSSION

1. What causes arguments between you and your loved one? Are these arguments winnable or even solvable?

2. How can you apply grace to these situations? Does it seem likely that this action will be successful?

ANSWERED PRAYER

Often when I pray, I wonder if my perception of my needs is correct. When I ask for help with a project, do I need help completing the project, or do I need to be reminded that the work I do is for God and not for me? If I pray to praise and thank God, am I actually thanking Him for what I think I earned on my own? Should I pray for relief from pain and illness, or should I pray for patience and endurance to suffer for Christ?

I suspect that most, if not all, of the time, my perspective on my situation is incorrect. I am especially reminded of this when I read Job. Job and his friends speculated on everything about Job's situation, from blame to rationale. When God speaks, we find He answers their argument by reminding us of His power, majesty, and glory. The truth in the Book of Job reminds me that God always answers our prayer, but He doesn't always answer our question as we pose it. Too often we ask the wrong question.

My prayer: Will You heal my loved one?

God's Word: "May the Lord direct your hearts to the love of God and to the steadfastness of Christ" (2 Thessalonians 3:5).

My prayer: Will You give me relief?

God's Word: "My grace is sufficient for you, for My power is made perfect in weakness" (2 Corinthians 12:9).

My prayer: Will You solve the confusion in my life?

God's Word: "The peace of God, which surpasses all understanding, will guard your hearts and your minds in Christ Jesus" (Philippians 4:7).

Often the questions we ask God show what happens when a perfect faith descends on a broken, sinful heart. Our sins bring doubt and confusion to our lives. God's answer redirected Job's despair and fear toward God's almighty power and wisdom. God did not focus on the questions debated by Job and his companions. Instead, He addressed the emotions that caused the questions and doubts.

We know that God always listens to and answers our prayers. When our limited perspective allows emotions to overwhelm us, God knows He must tend to our spiritual needs. Once He has restored our trust in Him, we can begin to accept that His perspective is best. Then our questions and doubts can fade into the peace of trust. Our God is steadfast in His love for us. When we suffer, when we grieve, when we are confused, this is the most important thing. God's answer to our prayer is always what we need.

PRAYER

Lord Jesus Christ, my life is full of struggle and confusion. My brain tries to make sense of the "what" and "whys" of things that happen. Remind me of Your steadfast love. Keep my mind and heart focused on You. Amen.

CHAPTER 23

ABIDE:
THE SUPPORT
OF HOSPICE CARE

As the Father has loved Me, so have I loved you. Abide in My love.

JOHN 15:9

It was a social media post from a former kindergarten student who is now a caregiver for the elderly. It was a simple post, but it was in no way typical. But then, this young lady is not typical either. She grew up in a family that taught her to care—and to care genuinely.

In the story, she was working to prepare a patient for moving to hospice. The job description asked her to clean and pack, but her heart asked her to pay attention to the man instead of his things. When she saw the look on his face, she sat beside him and took hold of his hand. She whispered to him that it was okay to leave. Slowly they breathed together until he breathed his last. She was fully present as his heart stopped beating and his struggle was over. God was with her as she set aside her chores to do the important work He put before her.

End-of-life care, often called hospice care, is an important topic that few people are eager to discuss. When we are healthy, we do not need to talk about it. When we are struggling with the possibility of a terminal illness, we delay this discussion because it makes us feel as if we have given up hope. When a loved one is finishing life's journey, we can be leery of bringing it up, preferring to let it sit like the proverbial "elephant in the room." We want to keep the discussion about death as a separate discussion from life, yet death is an inevitable part of life.

Let's face this discussion head-on by tackling some myths about end-of-life care.

- **It does not mean you are giving up hope.** There are two kinds of hope in the Christian life: "God will" and "God has already done." When struggling with an illness or a disabling condition, we are well aware of the "God will" kind of hope. We pray that God will grant healing and relief. We hope that God answers our prayer in the way we desire, granting relief from pain and suffering in the present world. This is an important kind of hope because it reminds us that God loves and cares for us in our present situation. However, the second kind of hope, the "God has already done" kind of hope, is the assurance of salvation earned through Jesus' death and resurrection. This is a hope placed in our hearts at our Baptism and rekindled each time we go to Holy Communion. The suffering we know now has no bearing on this hope. Our suffering does not mean God loves us less; instead, our suffering becomes a part of our longing for heaven. When you talk about death, you are not giving up hope for life. You are simply shifting your hope to the profound truth of eternal life.

- **It does not mean you are hurrying your loved one toward death.** When a young couple discusses bringing a child into the world, it does not necessarily mean that they intend to get pregnant right away. It is essential to have those critical planning discussions about work, child care, finances, and so forth before decisions are necessary. The same goes for discussions regarding hospice or end-of-life care, even if you are unsure you will need it in the near future. Conversations about "where," "how," and "who" can happen before you know the answer to the question of "when." See the Resources section for a tool to help you with this discussion ("Hospice Care Discussion," p. 194).

- **It does not mean you are doing the planning for God.** God's desire for His children happens as He determines, regardless of our plans. God will not decide to bring your loved one home earlier because you are talking about death. Furthermore, it is not God's will for us to be frightened of this part of our lives, as He is involved in every aspect of what happens to us from the beginning of time. Death is necessary but not permanent.

We do not need to make ourselves ready to die. Death will happen regardless. Christ has made us fit to be presented to God. God has planned for both the spiritual and physical processes involved in our death. He plans to give both comfort and hope. Death is not what God intended for His people; it is the result of our sin. Neither our fear nor our preparation will overcome death. When fear creeps into our thinking, we cling to the assurance that Christ has defeated death on our behalf. Talking about death can remind us of this hope and can offer comfort and peace to our loved ones when the time comes.

Let's think about the truth about hospice care.

- **Hospice care is supportive, not intrusive.** Hospice is not designed to come swooping in to tell you how to do things. The philosophy of hospice is to provide the support necessary to allow the process of death to follow its path. Hospice personnel have seen many families travel this journey. This enables them to see that there is not one right way to do this, but there are many good ways to support the process. Their interest is in finding ways to help you and your loved one, not direct the process or make decisions. Hospice abides. They wait with you and patiently for you, all of the time paying attention to needs they can answer.

- **Hospice support is physical, medical, educational, and emotional.** Hospice personnel will handle heavy tasks such as moving a loved one to assure comfort. They can communicate quickly with primary health-care providers, resulting in effective treatment changes. They possess a wealth of knowledge about end-of-life care and can explain what is happening and what to expect. This expertise does much to bring calm to those who are sitting with the loved one. A hospice worker has seen death and grief before, which allows him or her the unique perspective of being able to understand what you are experiencing. Even though they do not grieve with you, hospice workers walk alongside you through the process.

- **Hospice allows families to be fully present for their loved one.** There are many details and decisions involved in the weeks preceding death. Hospice workers are well trained to know what is necessary and when. This care lifts the burden from your shoulders. This service helps you to attend to your loved one and be fully present. Not only is this important for your loved one during the process of death, but it is also important for you once your loved one has passed. This time you spent together will be precious as you begin your journey of grief.

In hospice care, death is a time of abiding, of waiting patiently. It is a time for prayer, for reading God's Word, and for the comfort of holding a loved one's hand.

FOR FURTHER DISCUSSION

1. What is your experience with hospice care?

2. What is your biggest worry regarding end-of-life care?

3. What blessings can you imagine from a hospice experience?

WE ARE NOT ALONE

Abide is a beautiful word that suggests a patient waiting. In the Bible verse that begins this chapter, Jesus tells us to abide in His love. Here God's love for us becomes a shelter from the world and its events. We are not responsible for building or maintaining this shelter—God's love is unconditional. This abiding blesses us.

When we abide in God's love, we know we will never die alone. Even if we are not present for the death of a loved one, we know that Christ is there, providing comfort and peace. As children of God, we cannot die alone.

In our life and in our death, God abides. He welcomes us to His Table with the gift of forgiveness. He waits patiently to bring us home and assures us that we die in Christ. He is our way, our truth, and our steadfast hope for eternal life (John 14:6).

PRAYER

Lord Jesus Christ, You do not want death, and neither do I. Bless me with the comfort that because of Your sacrificial love, death cannot deny me eternal life with You. Amen.

CHAPTER 24

PURPOSE: WHEN DEATH BRINGS A NEW BEGINNING

But we do not want you to be uninformed, brothers, about those who are asleep, that you may not grieve as others do who have no hope. For since we believe that Jesus died and rose again, even so, through Jesus, God will bring with Him those who have fallen asleep.

1 THESSALONIANS 4:13–14

"We cannot call these trees beautiful because we must call them splendid."

These words make up my favorite quote from Dorris. She loved trees. She planted many around the family home and fought to save trees that were in danger of being cut down. She wrote a regular column on trees for the local newspaper, and she worked with her hometown so that it would be designated a Tree City USA through the Arbor Day Foundation (Tree City USA, Arbor Day Foundation, www.arborday.org/programs/treeCityUSA/index .cfm). And I remember the funeral home director mentioning her fierce love of trees as we met to plan her service. I have always thought that it was one of the blessings of her dementia diagnosis that during a drive, she could forget everything and simply enjoy the trees.

Dorris loved God's creation and saw planting, saving, and fighting for trees as a big part of her life's purpose. She also saw herself as a caregiver, having provided long-distance care for both of her parents and in-home care for her husband for many years of her life.

When God gives us the opportunity to provide care for a loved one, the aspects of care that fill our thoughts, actions, and days develop into our purpose. This purpose can come to define how we view ourselves. Our identity centers on being a child of God, but we carry earthly labels too. We are children, siblings, spouses, and parents. In addition to these labels, we understand ourselves through our skills. Maybe we are good with numbers or words and label ourselves as accountants, statisticians, authors, or speakers. Possibly we are teachers, pastors, managers, laborers, health-care professionals, or business owners. All of these labels come to define how we see ourselves and our place in the world. When one of these labels no longer applies, we must redefine our understanding of our purpose. This change is part of our grieving when we have lost someone or something dear to us.

- I lost my job, so I am no longer an employee.
- My wife left me, so I am no longer a spouse.
- My children are adults; am I still a parent?
- My physical, cognitive, or mental health is compromised; do I still have a purpose in this world?

- My loved one died, and I am no longer a caregiver. What is my purpose now?

Each of these situations involves the grief of loss and the grief of change. We do not slip into a new identity or purpose any more naturally than we grieve the loss of someone dear to us. When a loved one we cared for dies, we feel both loss and lost. We experience the loss of the loved one who was a significant part of our life. We also feel lost because the significant changes in our life leave us feeling at loose ends.

It is easy for non-caregivers to assume that once a loved one has died, there must be, mingled in with the grief, a sense of relief because of the release from caregiving. Before my family took on the role of caregivers, I had no understanding of how much space caregiving takes up in one's life. Yes, there is the time factor along with the extra responsibility, but caregiving becomes a much bigger part of your life and purpose than just that. For the duration of your caregiving, the loved one you cared for was an essential priority in your life. It is unlikely that this was your only priority, but it often superseded other concerns. You probably weighed the needs of your loved one before making any decision. Always, as you worked, you needed to think about how to communicate information and choices to others who were concerned about your loved one. If you were away, your thoughts and concerns were likely still focused on caregiving. And if you provided care for an extended period, you might find it difficult to separate yourself from the identity of being a caregiver. It is okay to feel lost. It is also okay to feel relief that the labor of caregiving has come to an end. God blesses us with new beginnings, and He equips us with the peace and strength to transition into those new beginnings.

It is also easy for non-caregivers to assume that the person who survives was the strong one, yet so often the person we care for was the one on whom we depended for courage and perseverance. We miss the wisdom, the strength, and the peace we found in that relationship. In addition to grieving, it is not unusual for the caregiver to experience fear—fear of change, of lack of purpose, of the future. And it is not unusual for the caregiver to feel anger about the loss of purpose, the loss of time spent providing care, or the inability to make things different for the care receiver.

Part of your purpose has been to obey God's call to love one another by sacrificing your wants and needs to be available for your loved one. This is an important pur- pose and a big part of your weary joy. Now that your loved one's struggle has ended in the promise of salvation, your work, life, and purpose will change, but your joy will con- tinue. Your joy will not replace your grief, but it will walk alongside it. We know this because our joy comes from God, and God is stronger than any fear, anger, or sadness we feel.

God's love for you will never change. As caregivers, we need to remember that we served our loved ones not to gain praise or acceptance, but rather out of gratitude to the God who redeemed us and gave us the opportunity to serve, and out of love and commitment to our care re- ceiver. Just as we do not provide care to earn a place in heaven, we also do not provide care to find our sense of worth in the world. When we no longer have the purpose of caregiving, we are not somehow suddenly less of a person. We are still precious children of God. Our heavenly Father cares about us, and He cares for us, and this is what defines us.

Years after my mother-in-law has passed away, I still think about her, and my brain still stops to check if there is something I should be doing. I have to prevent myself from turning the corner into her former memory care community, and I still have to remind myself that there are no more doctor appointments, check-ins with nursing staff, or emails to write to relatives. It is as if caregiving is still an open app in my brain. The situation is complicated further when I realize that I am still a caregiver, along with my siblings, for my parents. Their needs are different but still important. It has taken awhile for my thoughts to redirect my purpose. This is a part of my grief too.

The last weeks of my father-in-law's life were full of confusion as he was no longer able to process where he was or what he was doing. Now I know he is in a place where everything makes perfect sense. When I visited Dorris shortly after we moved her into the memory care facility, she greeted me with the words "I am so glad to see you because no one knows me here." Now she is in a place where she is completely known and completely loved. I would never wish for them to return to the lives they left. Instead, I treasure my memories and ask God to show me what will be His next purpose for each of us who provided care.

1. How has caregiving come to define your life?

2. What plans do you think God has for your future?

3. What specific comfort do you seek from God?

GRIEVING WITH HOPE

I remember a particular year when I was teaching kindergarten when a student in the class lost a parent to cancer. The idea of death was a mystery for this young student and her peers. During playtime they developed an interesting game where they would build a box, a child would get in the box, and the lid would be closed for a brief moment before the box was opened and the child emerged. The children played this game nearly every day. They found many different ways to build the box, but the game remained the same. As their teacher, I realized they were making a coffin as they tried to understand the concept of death. The game worried me until I realized something significant: each time they role-played death, they also role-played resurrection. God gave their play a double purpose.

For those of us who mourn the loss of a loved one, God brings us comfort for our grief and peace regarding our purpose and that of our loved one. We belong to Him, and we are a part of His plan. We do not grieve without hope. The hope we have is not a fingers-crossed, glass-half-full kind of hope. Our hope is assured. Christ's death and resurrection have already accomplished our hope for salvation. Our hope to see our loved one in heaven is not an uncertainty; it is a promise that waits for us.

God has been with you on your caregiving journey. He has provided you with wisdom, strength, and weary joy. His care for you will not stop now. Rest in this assurance: you are loved.

PRAYER

Lord Jesus Christ, I offer a prayer of gratitude that You have fitted me for this purpose. Please be with other caregivers I know and love, and help me to share Your strength and peace with them. Hold me in Your hand, surround me with Your love, bless me with Your peace. Amen.

RESOURCES

INFORMATION FOR HEALTH-CARE PROVIDERS

Your patient has been diagnosed with a form of dementia. Please consider the following guidelines to provide better and more efficient care.

1. Even though your patient may be able to recite his or her birth date and Social Security number, this does not mean he or she can answer your questions about a fall or even current symptoms. He or she does not remember recent events, and his or her responses to questions may be a compilation of memories.

2. Do not ask questions of your patient while he or she is walking, climbing onto the examination table, or turning. Such actions are no longer automatic for your patient and take all available cognition.

3. Please don't ask your patient about medical history or medicine lists. The care facility or the loved one accompanying the patient has provided paperwork showing current prescriptions and dosages. The patient may be able to verify, but keep in mind that a memory care patient will likely say yes when the correct answer can no longer be retrieved from memory.

4. Don't ask broad or vague questions such as "Do you need anything?" Your patient will get lost trying to find an answer. Instead, ask about a specific need.

5. Do not separate a memory care patient from a loved one. This person represents all that is familiar in this stressful environment and can rephrase your questions in a way that your patient can answer. Make sure all medical information is shared in the presence of a family member.

6. While for most patients, small talk can be soothing, for a memory care patient it merely adds more stress because it leaves the patient struggling for responses and wondering if he or she knows you. Even though it feels awkward, it is a good idea to say your name, occupation, and reason for being there each time you enter the room.

CAREGIVER HEALTH INVENTORY

Use this chart to take time to consider your situation and your health needs as caregiver. Share this with a loved one who can take time to look out for you. Your answers to these questions will also be informative for your own health-care provider. It is a good idea to keep your physician informed of your circumstances, should you need advice specific to your situation.

CAREGIVER HEALTH INVENTORY

ASK YOURSELF	ANSWERS	HOW CAN YOU COUNTERACT THESE CONSEQUENCES?
Has your financial health changed since becoming a caregiver? Do you have new worries in this area? Do you have long-term concerns?		

Has your physical health changed? Are you sleeping well? Do you quickly recover from viruses? Do you have regular medical checkups, at least once a year?		
What coping strategies have you successfully used in the past? Are you able to continue them as a caregiver?		
Has your emotional health changed? Do you feel more tired than usual? Do your emotions feel flat? How do you handle anxiety? Do you have someone you can talk with and pray with on a regular basis?		
What activities that you enjoyed in the past have you given up because of caregiving? What did you enjoy about those activities? Have you found a new way to bring enjoyment into your life?		
How comfortable are you with asking for help? What stops you? What encourages you?		
Whom do you know that could provide even a little help for you? Is it family members? friends? your pastor? other professionals such as counselors, nurses, or social workers? List as many people as you can and what help they might be able to offer.		

SAFETY CHECKUP

Use this chart as you consider the safety needs of your situation as a caregiver. Fill it out with other family members who can add their own concerns and observations and so they can understand your needs. Share this with your primary health-care provider for more insights and ideas.

ISSUE TO CONSIDER	PERSONAL NOTES
Mobility ☐ Is there safe mobility throughout the house and between the house and the car? ☐ Is the live-in caregiver physically able to provide the needed assistance? ☐ If there were a fall, would someone be able to help physically? ☐ In the instance of memory challenges, is the loved one adequately contained within a safe area? ☐ If a memory-challenged loved one were to wander off, would those in the neighborhood know what to do?	
Equipment ☐ Is there adequate equipment to create safe areas in the bathroom, bedroom, living room, and kitchen? ☐ Has the risk of a memory-challenged loved one starting a fire or causing other damage been eliminated? ☐ Can all caregivers safely and effectively operate all necessary medical equipment?	
Assistance ☐ Are medications being taken consistently? ☐ Are meals being eaten consistently? ☐ Are hygiene needs being met consistently? ☐ Are doctor appointments being kept?	

Discernment ☐ Is the care receiver vulnerable to scams via mail or phone? ☐ Do you trust the care receiver's decision-making capabilities? ☐ Are financial decisions an issue? ☐ If there is a live-in caregiver (such as a spouse), does this person have everything necessary to provide proper care? ☐ Does this person have respite care to allow for personal needs to be met?	

HEALTH-CARE INFORMATION CHECKLIST

☐ **Medications**	Nearly every health-care provider will ask for a medication list, even for medicine they have a record of providing. It is a good sign when providers double-check this information. Create a list that includes both prescription medications and other treatments, such as vitamins, herbal supplements, and over-the-counter allergy or pain medications. Your pharmacist is an excellent resource for information regarding treatments and possible drug interactions.
☐ **Previous surgeries, facility stays, or critical medical events**	The more frequently medical events happen, the more challenging it is to keep them all straight. A timeline that includes any of these events is valuable information for a health-care provider.
☐ **Insurance cards**	It is worth it to go to a copy center and get all insurance cards, Medicare, and Medicaid cards copied front and back on one sheet. Then make copies of these for registration or checking in.
☐ **Identification**	If your loved one no longer has a valid driver's license, it is worth the challenges to get a government-issued ID. Keep a copy of this in your file in case an emergency causes the ID to be left behind.
☐ **Advanced directives**	A signed DNR does not lock you into a decision, but care communities want to be clear on your preferences. Likewise, they will want a copy of a living will and power of attorney for health care and financial oversight. An advanced directive means that you and your loved one will have made your wishes known with regard to decisions about end-of-life care.

BIBLE PASSAGES
FOR COMFORT AND PEACE

Bible Verse	Comforting Truth
In peace I will both lie down and sleep; for You alone, O LORD, make me dwell in safety. *Psalm 4:8* It is through God's strength that I can have peace. His peace is stronger than my grief or anger.	**PEACE**
The LORD is near to the brokenhearted and saves the crushed in spirit. *Psalm 34:18* God knows when we are frustrated or despondent. He sends comfort.	**COMFORT**
When the righteous cry for help, the LORD hears and delivers them out of all their troubles. *Psalm 34:17* God's best deliverance is to calm our fears. His protection is always with us.	**PROTECTION**
The LORD your God is in your midst, a mighty one who will save; He will rejoice over you with gladness; He will quiet you by His love; He will exult over you with loud singing. *Zephaniah 3:17* God's care for us is complete. He saves us, delights in us, and quiets us.	**CARE**
Come to Me, all who labor and are heavy laden, and I will give you rest. Take My yoke upon you, and learn from Me, for I am gentle and lowly in heart, and you will find rest for your souls. *Matthew 11:28–29* God provides us with rest and renewed strength when we feel we can no longer continue.	**REST**
In Him we live and move and have our being. *Acts 17:28* Even when we feel alone, we know that God is with us.	**PRESENCE**

In quietness and in trust shall be your strength. *Isaiah 30:15b* Our strength is found not within us, but in our God-given trust.	**STRENGTH**
When the cares of my heart are many, Your consolations cheer my soul. *Psalm 94:19* God takes away our worries and replaces them with His joy.	**CONSOLATION**
I do not cease to give thanks for you, remembering you in my prayers. *Ephesians 1:16* Our gratitude reminds us of how God helps us.	**GRATITUDE**
We love because [God] first loved us. *1 John 4:19* God's love gives us the strength to love others in all circumstances.	**LOVE**
See what kind of love the Father has given to us, that we should be called children of God; and so we are. *1 John 3:1a* Our needs are important to God.	**VALUE**
Those who sow in tears shall reap with shouts of joy! *Psalm 126:5* It is God's will that we know His joy.	**JOY**
The LORD will keep your going out and your coming in from this time forth forevermore. *Psalm 121:8* The Lord is always protecting us.	**PROTECTION**
Am I a God at hand, declares the LORD, and not a God far away? *Jeremiah 23:23* God is not a distant figure. He is with us.	**NEARNESS**
Let Your steadfast love, O LORD, be upon us, even as we hope in You. *Psalm 33:22* Our hope comes from our salvation.	**HOPE**
The LORD has heard my plea; the LORD accepts my prayer. *Psalm 6:9* God does not wait for us to pray to Him. He knows what we need.	**INTERCESSION**

We were buried therefore with Him by baptism into death, in order that, just as Christ was raised from the dead by the glory of the Father, we too might walk in newness of life. *Romans 6:4*	**BELONGING**
We are precious members of the family of God.	

HOSPICE CARE DISCUSSION

Use these categories and questions to guide your discussions about end-of-life care. Use the questions that make sense to you and your loved one. Take time to spread them out over several meetings. Over time, the answers may change, but the discussion will be time well spent.

Which service will provide care?	
1. Ask your pastor for recommendations, given the likelihood that he has worked with several organizations.	
2. Check into the hospice options available in your area. Can they come to your home? Do they offer services at a dedicated hospice facility? Can they provide services at another care facility? Does the current care facility allow a separate hospice service to work there?	
Where will the care be provided?	
1. Hospice can happen at home or at a facility. What is the preference and why?	

2. Does this site work well for the caregiver (allowing for respite) and for the family (enough room)?	

How can the care be personalized?	
1. What resources do you have at home or in the area? Books? Friends? Family?	
2. What Bible passages and hymns bring you the most comfort in your daily life?	
3. What life mementos/photographs are especially meaningful to you?	

Why does the care happen in this way?	
1. What questions do you have for your primary health-care provider?	
2. What questions do you have for the hospice-care provider?	
3. What questions do you have for other family members regarding their wishes or worries?	

When should people be notified?	
1. At what point do you want hospice to come?	
2. At what point do you plan to inform family?	
3. What information will be shared with family and friends?	
4. Do you want a large family gathering while there is enough energy to enjoy interaction?	
5. Would you prefer quiet individual visits?	
6. Do you prefer scheduled visits, or are drop-ins okay?	

What issues are there to resolve?	
1. What important conversations still need to happen?	
2. How and when will these conversations occur?	
3. Who can help?	

SOURCES

Barba, G. Dalla, and M.-F. Boissé. "Temporal Consciousness and Confabulation: Is the Medial Temporal Lobe 'Temporal'?" *Cognitive Neuropsychiatry* 15, no. 1 (January 2010): 95–117.

"Caregiver Isolation and Loneliness." Family Caregiver Alliance; National Center on Caregiving, last modified September 20, 2012, www.caregiver.org/caregiver-isolation-and-loneliness.

Chappell, Neena, and Laura M. Funk. "Social Support, Caregiving, and Aging." *Canadian Journal on Aging* 30, no. 3 (2011): 355–70.

Collier, Roger. "Hospital-Induced Delirium Hits Hard." *Canadian Medical Association Journal* 184, no. 1 (January 2012): 23–24.

"Controlling Anger before It Controls You." American Psychological Association (2018) www.apa.org/topics/anger/control.aspx.

Covinsky, Kenneth E., R. Newcomer, P. Fox, J. Wood, L. Sands, K. Dane, and K. Yaffe. "Patient and Caregiver Characteristics Associated with Depression in Caregivers of Patients with Dementia." *Journal of General Internal Medicine* 18 (December, 2003): 1006–14.

Davidai, Shai, and T. Gilovich. "The Headwinds/Tailwinds Asymmetry: An Availability Bias in Assessments of Barriers and Blessings." *Journal of Personality and Social Psychology* 111, no. 6 (December 2016): 835–51.

"Depression (Major Depressive Disorder)." Mayo Clinic, last modified February 3, 2018, www.mayoclinic.org/diseases-conditions/depression/symptoms-causes/syc-20356007.

Feil, Naomi. *The Validation Breakthrough: Simple Techniques for Communicating with People with Alzheimer's-Type Dementia.* Towson, Md.: Health Professions Press, 2002.

Fredrickson, Barbara. *Love 2.0: Creating Happiness and Health in Moments of Connection.* New York: Plume, 2013.

Ghent-Fuller, Jennifer. *Understanding the Dementia Experience, Book I.* Thoughtful Dementia Care, Inc., 2012.

Grandey, Alicia. "Emotion Regulation in the Workplace: A New Way to Conceptualize Emotional Labor." *Journal of Occupational Healthy Psychology* 5, no. 1 (2000): 95–110.

Heerema, Esther, and Claudia Chaves. "Using Validation Therapy for People with Dementia." VerywellHealth, last modified August 01, 2017, www.verywellhealth.com/using-validation-therapy-for-people-with-dementia-98683.

Hughes, Margaret. "A Strengths Perspective on Caregiving at the End-of-Life." *Australian Social Work* 68, no. 2 (2015): 156.

Jacobsen, Juliet C., Guy Maytal, and Theodore A. Stern. "Demoralization in Medical Practice." *The Primary Care Companion to the Journal of Clinical Psychiatry* 9, no. 2 (2007): 139–43.

Plass, Ewald M., comp. *What Luther Says: A Practical In-Home Anthology for the Active Christian.* St. Louis: Concordia Publishing House, 1959.

"Understanding the Stress Response: Chronic Activation of This Survival Mechanism Impairs Health." Harvard Health Publishing: Harvard Medical School, last modified May 1, 2018, www.health.harvard.edu/staying-healthy/understanding-the-stress-response.

Wilkins, Julia, and Amy Janel Eisenbraun. "Humor Theories and the Physiological Benefits of Laughter." *Holistic Nursing Practice* 23, no. 6 (November–December 2009): 349–54.

Winerman, Lea. "The Mind's Mirror." *Monitor* 36, no. 9 (October 2005): 48, www.apa.org/monitor/oct05/mirror.aspx.